THE HEGEL VARIATIONS

THE HEGEL VARIATIONS

On the *Phenomenology of Spirit*

———◆———

FREDRIC JAMESON

VERSO

London • New York

First published by Verso 2010
Copyright © Fredric Jameson 2010
All rights reserved

1 3 5 7 9 10 8 6 4 2

Verso
UK: 6 Meard Street, London W1F 0EG
US: 20 Jay Street, Suite 1010, Brooklyn, NY 11201
www.versobooks.com

Verso is the imprint of New Left Books

ISBN-13: 978-1-84467-616-3

British Library Cataloguing in Publication Data
A catalogue record for this book is available from the British Library

Library of Congress Cataloging-in-Publication Data
A catalog record for this book is available from the Library of Congress

Typeset in Garamond by Hewer Text UK Ltd, Edinburgh
Printed in the United States by Maple Vail

For ripi

Contents

Chapter I

Closure

Let's begin with the ending: it is above all else urgent not to think of "Absolute Spirit" as a "moment," whether historical or structural or even methodological. Absolute Spirit cannot be considered as a terminus of any kind, without transforming the whole of *Phenomenology of Spirit* into a developmental narrative,[1] one that can be characterized variously as teleological or cyclical, but which in either case is to be vigorously repudiated by modern, or at least by contemporary, thought of whatever persuasion.

Is it, then, to be thought of as the final unveiling of the dialectic (a word Hegel uses very sparingly indeed), or perhaps as the definitive inauguration of something Hegel is much more frequently willing to call the "speculative"? These descriptions have their kernel of truth, insofar as the great movement from *Verstand* or Understanding to *Vernunft* or Reason is grasped as a radical break with common-sense empiricism and with what we may also call reified thinking. In the *Logic*, however, the cancellation and transformation of *Verstand* (and this really may be considered an *Aufhebung*) is followed by not one but two moments, either of which might be called dialectical, albeit

---

[1] It has been rumored that the formal paradigm for Hegel's *Bildungsroman* was *La Vie de Marianne* of Marivaux (1731–1745): see Jacques d'Hondt, "Hegel et Marivaux," in *Europe*, vol. 44, December 1966, 323–337. For d'Hondt, however, the kinship lies less in the sequence of episodes than in Marianne's achievement of a truly divided self-consciousness.

for somewhat different reasons. The second part of both *Logic*s (the "greater" Logic of 1812–1816 as well as the smaller "Encyclopedia" Logic of 1817) is entitled Essence and deals with "reflection" or what we would call binary oppositions—in other words, very specifically what earns the term "unity of opposites," a dialectical matter indeed. The third or final part, however, that is devoted to the Notion or *Begriff,* is a more metaphysical (or "speculative") affirmation of the ultimate unity of subject and object, of the I and the not-I or nature, a unity that can take either the form of the syllogism or that of Life.[2] What ultimately makes both of these kinds of thinking unsuitable candidates for constituting a whole new historical era or moment is the persistence of *Verstand* within them as the ongoing and inevitable thinking of everyday life and a material world.

It is certain that Hegel is what might anachronistically be called an ideologist of the modern,[3] and that he thinks that a whole new conceptual (and political) practice characterizes his own period (whether one begins that with the French Revolution or Kant, or with Luther and the Reformation). But it is not so clear whether for Hegel the new post-revolutionary and constitutional populations have achieved truly dialectical enlightenment. The judgment is bound up with that of the status of his philosophy: is it truly universal and exoteric, or rather an esoteric doctrine accessible only

---

[2] According to Althusser, Lenin retains the second stage of the Hegelian progression ("the determinations of reflection") while abandoning the more idealist dimensions of the Notion itself (in the syllogism and Life): see Louis Althusser, "Lenin before Hegel," in *Lenin and Philosophy,* trans. Ben Brewster, New York: Monthly Review Press, 1971, 113. I tend to agree with this preference, but would rather substitute ideology for idealism. As for life, Hegel's version of it, pre-Darwinian as it is, is probably far too metaphysical and epistemological (highest form of the unity of subject and object) to be of much interest for us today. Still we might give Hegel credit for the first timid step in the direction of that vitalism which, a mighty stream from Nietzsche and Tolstoy through D. H. Lawrence to Deleuze, has been so energizing a worldview (which is to say, ideology) in contemporary thought.

[3] I take it that this is the position of Robert Pippin, *Modernism as a Philosophical Problem*, Oxford: Blackwell, 1991; and see also below.

to the happy few? I would suggest that the turning point in Hegel's judgment on that status is to be located in his first teaching year in the Nuremberg *Gymnasium*, when he finds to his dismay that the *Phenomenology* is not a satisfactory guide for his students after all, and concludes that philosophy cannot realistically be part of the high school curriculum as he once thought (a disillusionment that significantly coincides with Napoleon's defeat, and a new reactionary hegemony over Europe).[4]

Still, might not the chapter on Absolute Spirit signal a different kind of historical inauguration, that of the appearance of a new kind of human being here and there among the general population—if not the Nietzschean superman, then at least what Kojève calls the Sage, whom he goes so far as to identify with the Platonic philosopher-king?[5] The momentary appearance of Napoleon on the world stage lends historical weight and interest to Kojève's interpretation. Yet it cannot be said that Hegel's conception of the "world-historical individual" reinforces Kojève's anthropomorphism, inasmuch as the very idea of the "ruse of reason or history" devalues the individual "great man" by demonstrating that he is merely a pawn or a tool in the hands of historical development. Kojève's view here is akin to the temptation of personification in literary analysis and traditional allegory, and certainly goes against the grain of the contemporary theory anxious to decenter the subject and to invent collective or structural analyses for what used to be individualizing ones. Indeed, nothing in the final chapter of the *Phenomenology* suggests Hegel's complicity in the idea of the Sage with which Kojève here endows him.

But surely Absolute Spirit may be seen as a kind of method, in a chapter which systematically reviews all the moments of the *Phenomenology* and characterizes their findings as truths "for us,"

---

[4] Terry Pinkard, *Hegel: A Biography*, Cambridge: Cambridge University Press, 2000, 323.

[5] Alexandre Kojève, *Introduction à la Lecture de Hegel*, Paris: Gallimard, 1947. Future references to this work are denoted *ILH*. Significantly, Allan Bloom's useful English abridgement omits the central political seminar of 1936–1937 (113–157).

and insights we have only been qualified to earn on the strength of reaching this final "speculative" conviction about the ultimate unity of subject and object? Yet the very concept of method flattens out all the properly dialectical differences between the chapters and screens out the stimulating heterogeneity of the *Phenomenology* itself. The dialectic is not enhanced by its association with the truly vulgar and instrumental idea of method, a temptation we would do well to resist but which is certainly reinforced by the omnipresence of *Verstand* or that reified thinking of which "method" is so striking an example.

What may well prove more congenial to a contemporary or a postmodern public is the invocation of Marx's notion of "General Intellect" (which has also been foundational for the Negri/Hardt theory of the multitude).[6] Marx's expression (found in the *Grundrisse*) evokes an historically new kind of general literacy in the mass public, most strikingly evinced in the trickling down of scientific knowledge (and technological know-how) in the population at large, a transformation that might also be described in terms of the displacement of a peasant (or feudal) mentality by a more general urban one (and in hindsight also comprehensible as a fundamental consequence of literacy and mass culture). At any rate, the hypothesis of such a social transformation in consciousness and mentality (in "Spirit" or *Geist* in Hegel's sense) is not at all incompatible with Hegel's narrative here; and it strengthens the renewed appeal of Hegel's work and the revival of interest in it, in a postmodernity characterized by cynical reason and by what I will later on term plebeianization.

We must at any rate read Absolute Spirit as a symptom rather than a prophecy, and thereby rescue the *Phenomenology* from its stereotypical reading as an out-of-date teleology. Indeed, in what follows I will argue that the "ladder of forms" of this work is as open-ended as one likes. How else to explain the persistence today of that

---

[6] Karl Marx, *Grundrisse*, London: Penguin, 1973, 706; and on the fortunes of this idea for contemporary Italian radicalism, see Paolo Virno, "General Intellect," in *Historical Materialism*, vol. 15 num. 3, 2007, 3–8.

opposition between left-Hegelians (such as Kojève) and right-Hegelians (Fukuyama and the triumph of American capitalism) that had already declared itself in the struggle for his system immediately after Hegel's own death?

Chapter 2

Organizational Problems

If indeed it still seems necessary to propose another reading of *Phenomenology of Spirit*, one that claims some difference from the seemingly innumerable studies of this work only partially conveyed by the most extensive bibliographies, this not only has to do with the relatively recent rediscovery and revival of interest in this book,[7] about which Hegel himself had mixed feelings later on in his career as he elaborated that "Hegelianism" which, as a philosophical system, would be synonymous with his name down to the 1930s. He himself meant it, as his tenure publication, to be a teaching manual; when in the Nuremberg gymnasium the effort proved a dismal failure (as I have already observed), he not only abandoned his commitment to the teaching of philosophy in the secondary schools, but began to plan new and far more systematic manuals—most notably the three-volume *Enzyklopädie*—which henceforth left the position of the *Phenomenology* in permanent doubt, for himself as well as for his followers: was it an introduction or propaedeutic to philosophy, something whose possibility its own *Vorwort* vigorously denies, or was it actually one constitutive part of that philosophy whose various panels—logic, aesthetics, political philosophy, science—seemed to leave no place for it?

---

[7] It would seem that even during Hegel's lifetime the *Phenomenology* was eclipsed by the *Logic* and the later Berlin writings and lectures only to be restored to its rightful place by Dilthey in the late nineteenth century.

Uncertainties of this kind are welcome in the way in which they expose the text to multiple possibilities of interpretation which cannot be resolved philologically. But what far more insistently calls for rereading and reinterpretation is the presence in this book of a number of themes which have seemed permanently relevant over the last century, despite or perhaps even because of the radical changes in the historical situations in which, as questions, they still insistently reappear: these are most notably the Master/Slave dialectic and the infamous "end of history" (but the Unhappy Consciousness and the "beautiful soul" are also still very much with us, along with a number of other conceptual markers, as I hope to demonstrate below).

Yet what endows these textual moments with renewed interest for us today is their form fully as much as their content: for the very heterogeneity of the book has prevented any one of them from being fully assimilated to some homogeneous dimension of philosophical thought and discourse. They have not been able to be transformed into pure or coherent philosophical positions, into identifiable ideas or concepts, into reified tokens about which we can say that they represent Hegel's official thoughts or his "positions" on this or that. Nor does this have to do with the much appreciated obscurity of his writing (as opposed to the relative lucidity of the lectures also taken down for us): Hegel's practice of the sentence will certainly detain us here; but it is in terms of his practice of the dialectic which these uncertainties have most often been rehearsed; and we need to be very vigilant about the way in which we evoke this mysterious entity, and in particular wary of its translation back into one of those purely philosophical concepts (the "unity of opposites," for example) that the dialectic itself came into being to forestall or interrupt, to displace or deconstruct, but also to set back in motion. Fortunately, the *Phenomenology* is itself far more vigilant in this respect than the later works, and not the least source of its famous difficulty will be not merely its reluctance to pronounce the word dialectic or to endow it with the density and substantiality of a name or a method, but also the complicated footwork with which it attempts to avoid taking positions at the same time that it expounds them.

This productive uncertainty about the philosophical status of the *Phenomenology* is matched by equally productive ambiguities or hesitations on other formal or organizational issues. It has for example been noted, practically since the first publication of the book in the triumphant Napoleonic years, that there is a gap and a division, not to speak of an opposition, between the first chapters, on consciousness, and the bulk of the later chapters, which professional philosophers are inclined to describe as sociological (when they do not simply deal with what can be designated as the "history of ideas"). It may be thought that Hegel himself attempted to mask or paper over this shift of registers by introducing a set of superimposed oppositions which certainly complicate this issue. Thus the Consciousness chapters are contrasted with a Self-consciousness section, followed by a section on Reason (*Vernunft*), which on one numeration (as C) completes the triad on consciousness, but on another (simultaneous) one (as AA) appears to oppose itself to Spirit (*der Geist*, BB), itself then followed by CC (Religion) and DD (Absolute Spirit), as though these four categories now formed yet a different kind of series.

It is certain that the large virtually self-sufficient panel on religion complicates the issue in ways I will discuss later on (while Absolute Spirit turns out to be little more than a summary of the book we have just read). At any rate, it is also clear that at least part of the Reason section ("observing reason") falls back into the purely philosophical classification insofar as it is a contribution to that subsection of philosophy called epistemology, while the preceding section on Self-consciousness (which contains the famous master/slave episode) would seem, as political philosophy, to anticipate the sociology/history-of-ideas category (into which its accompanying panel on stoicism, skepticism and the Unhappy Consciousness still more clearly falls).

The first three chapters seem relatively self-contained, and to pursue an identifiable and more technically philosophical argument, which runs from the immediacy of purely physical sensation (the here and now) to the first discovery of scientific law, as an abstraction behind and beyond that sensory experience. Famously the first chapter uses language to undermine the seeming immediacy of the sense; the second observes the reorganization of the sensory world into the perception of objects which function as containers for their various properties; the third finally pushes on into some ultimate restructuration in which the physical experience of the world becomes inessential in the light of the unseen and imperceptibly abstract scientific laws posited behind it (Hegel characterizes them famously as an "inverted world" lying beyond and behind this one).

Still, there can be little doubt that the overall division marks a shift of registers, and that each group has given rise to a distinctive set of commentaries. The initial philosophical chapters have been seen as Hegel's solution to the problems with which Kant's work left the younger German philosophical generation, with its intent to move from mere epistemology à la Kant to full-throated metaphysics or ontology, beginning with Fichte. These problems turn mostly around the opposition between subject and object and their relationship, which Kant had left in a kind of provisional limbo (we can know our knowledge of things but not the "things-in-themselves"). Fichte boldly emerges from this methodological suspension by affirming the very production of the object by the subject, followed in this by Schelling's daring and comprehensive exploration of what he called the philosophy of Nature.

Will we then still want to say that Hegel then reinstates the subject itself in this discussion? His programmatic formula, Subject or System, would seem to confirm this characterization, at the same time that it opens the door to all those vibrant contemporary arguments about Hegel's relations with Spinoza and the latter's alleged superiority to him (immediately reintroducing the issue of temporality and therewith of the dialectic, both presumably absent from Spinoza).[8]

But it is more appropriate to say that Hegel sublates the dilemma of subject and object by projecting a new dimension of thinking, called *speculative*, which presupposes their identity in advance, and

---

[8] See for a measured position on the Spinoza/Hegel opposition, Pierre Macherey, *Hegel ou Spinoza*, Paris: Maspero, 1979.

which will later on authorize the deployment of that whole immense Hegelian system whose multiple sub-programs scarcely dwindle by comparison with Aristotle himself, in this respect Hegel's great model and master.

As for the contemporary discussions and commentaries on these technical philosophical debates, I will hazard the impression that the rich tradition of postwar German scholarship, from Dieter Henrich on, has tended to move backwards to reclaim Schelling, and even to produce a fourth philosophical partner in what is no longer a triumvirate, in the person of the poet Friedrich Hölderlin, whose early writings are alleged to have affirmed the unity of subject and object in advance, thereby rendering Hegel's laborious climb to the speculative unnecessary.[9]

Meanwhile, a growing body of distinguished American philosophy, centered on the work of Robert Pippin, and baptizing this whole complex of technical philosophical problems and solutions "post-Kantian," has tended to revindicate the dignity of the old label of idealism, fallen into some disrepute in the post-war period. It is a move which has some plausibility in the midst of the current Bergson revival, even though its arguments about consciousness and the limits consciousness set for philosophy have little enough in common with Deleuzian and virtualist theorizing.[10]

Pippin has taught us to reread Hegel's arguments with the respect due a rigorous philosophizing, even though he achieves this by a modest lowering of the volume of Hegel's dialectical claims, which are surely what have always excited the latter's followers, not many of whom will be altogether content with the unpretentious Rortyan pragmatism of this new avatar.

But this rescue operation, which makes Hegel respectable and allows him reentry into the fraternity of professional philosophers, has a consequence which elementary dialectics might have predicted

---

[9] This is, I take it, the burden of Dieter Henrich's work on objective idealism: see "Hegel und Hölderlin," in *Hegel Im Kontext*, Frankfurt: Suhrkamp, 1971; and also *Between Kant and Hegel*, Cambridge: Harvard University Press, 2003.
[10] But see Gilles Deleuze, *Le Bergsonisme*, Paris: PUF, 1966.

in advance, namely—and as a result of the reaffirmation of the rigor of the philosophical chapters—the slippage of the non-philosophical (or "sociological") chapters into the impressionistic flabbiness of a generalizing "culture critique." The Americans have tried to forestall this unfortunate development by lending Hegel contemporary relevance as a philosopher of modernity; and insofar as the epithet directs our attention to the more immediate cultural problems of Napoleonic and post-revolutionary society the effort is meritorious. But it cannot long block the downward rush; and when "modernity" comes to be endowed with all the familiar Nietzschean and existential characteristics—death of god, end of values, alienation, etc.—Hegel's originality as a thinker evaporates (along with his relevance to the postmodern age, for which none of these "problems" are any longer an issue).

This is why the most useful and productive commentaries on the second (or sociological) batch of *Phenomenology* chapters are rather those elaborated from a political and indeed a Marxist perspective, in which even the status of what gets called culture or cultural is profoundly modified. The fountainhead of such commentary is of course the classic lecture series of Alexandre Kojève in the 1930s, still stimulating, but about which I think some new kinds of questions can now be raised.

For the moment I will merely lay down a rough and general framework for grasping the organizational fault line responsible for the emergence of these various philosophical and political traditions. It seems to me that things fall into place if we follow Hegel himself in his peremptory definition of Spirit or *Geist* as "the ethical life of a nation [das sittliche Leben eines Volkes] insofar as it is the immediate truth—the individual that is a world."[11]

---

[11] G. W. F. Hegel, *Werke*, vol. 3, Frankfurt: Suhrkamp, 1971–1979, 326; in English, *Phenomenology of Spirit*, trans. A. V. Miller, Oxford: Oxford University Press, 1977, 265. Unless otherwise noted, all page numbers provided in the text refer to this work; all page references will cite the German edition first, followed by the English translation; when only one set of page numbers is present they refer to the language edition in which the text is provided.

In this fundamental identification of *Geist* with collectivity I have followed the movement of Adorno's thinking in his first Hegel essay, which reaches its climax at the utterly unexpected eruption of the Marx of the 1844 manuscripts. Yet this high point is also, characteristically, the moment at which we begin our downward path towards everything ideological in Hegelian idealism. What is remarkable is that at the very moment at which Adorno names the content of *Geist* or Spirit as *Gesellschaft* or society, he abruptly withdraws the identification, or at least its terminological articulation:

> The interpretation of spirit as society, accordingly, appears to be . . . incompatible with the sense of Hegel's philosophy if only because it does not satisfy the precept of immanent criticism and attempts to grasp the truth content of Hegelian philosophy in terms of something external to it, something that his philosophy, within its own framework, would have derived as conditioned or posited. Explicit critique of Hegel, of course, could show that he was not successful in that deduction. The linguistic expression "existence," which is necessarily conceptual, is confused with what it designates, which is nonconceptual, something that cannot be melted down into identity.

> Die Deutung von Geist als Gesellschaft erscheint demnach als unvereinbar mit dem Sinn der Hegelschsen Philosophie allein schon darum, weil sie sich gegen die Maxime immanenter Kritik verfehle, den Wahrheitsgehalt der Hegelschen Philosophie an einem ihr Äußerlichen zu ergreifen suche, das diese in ihrem eigenen Gefüge als Bedingtes oder Gesetztes abgeleitet habe. Die explizite Hegelkritik freilich könnte dartun, daß jene Deduktion ihm nicht gelang. Der sprachliche Ausdruck Existenz, notwendig ein Begriffliches, wird verwechselt mit dem, was er designiert, dem Nichtbegrifflichen, in Identität nicht Einzuschmelzenden.[12]

Yes, Spirit is the collective, but we must not call it that, owing to the reification of language, owing to the positivities of the

---

[12] Theodor Adorno, *Hegel: Three Studies*, trans. Shierry Weber Nicholsen, Cambridge: The MIT Press, 1993, 19; *Drei Studien zu Hegel*, in *Gesammelte Schriften*, Frankfurt: Suhrkamp, 1997, 5:266.

philosophical terms or names themselves, which restore precisely that empirical common-sense ideology it was the very vocation of the dialectic to destroy in the first place. To name the social is to make it over into a thing or an empirical entity, just as to celebrate its objectivity in the face of idealistic subjectivism is to reestablish the old subject-object opposition which was to have been done away with. A similar, profoundly Adornian move can be observed in his next step (in which I also follow him).

As always in Hegel, however, the term "immediate" is a warning signal: indeed, the whole of Hegel's philosophical production is an elaborate refutation of all possible concepts of immediacy. He therefore continues:

> It [Spirit] must advance to the consciousness of what it is immediately, must leave behind it the beauty of ethical life [das schöne sittliche Leben], and by passing through a series of shapes [Gestalten] attain to a knowledge of itself. These shapes, however, are distinguished from the previous ones by the fact that they are real Spirits, actualities in the strict meaning of the word [this whole phrase is Miller's paraphrase of eigentliche Wirklichkeiten], and instead of being shapes merely of consciousness, are shapes of a world. (326; 265)

We can disambiguate Hegel's discussions by holding firm to the principle that the words Spirit or *Geist*, wherever they appear, have nothing to do with spirituality nor even with consciousness itself as such (whose philosophical problems have already been sharply differentiated by Hegel himself in his organizational scheme). I would even go so far as to say that Spirit means nothing cultural, in the looser sense in which that word is generally used (but I will come back to that sense later on; the problem is a central one for my reading). We must, in other words, hold firmly to the conviction that in Hegel the word "Spirit" always designates the collective, a second word I use as a more neutral one than society, which immediately raises substantive and historical problems. When we do so I believe we will find that many false problems fall away: thus the peculiar emplacement of observing Reason outside the Spirit chapters, and in seeming opposition to them, can be explained by the hypothesis that for Hegel scientific research—here the paradigm of Reason—is an individual pursuit, and not (or not yet) a marker of the quality of this or that historical moment in the development of society.

Indeed, Reason is here explicitly identified with empiricism (144; 184), and a host of figures of forgetting ("after losing the grave of its truth, after the abolition of its actuality is itself abolished" [140; 179]) underscore its own necessary forgetfulness of its own evolution out of the Unhappy Consciousness ("it has this path behind it and has forgotten it" [141; 180]). What has been forgotten is essentially the Other, and the structure of self-consciousness which the shock of the other produces/reveals; so that its discovery of the Categories (which confirm the unity of consciousness and the not-I), its "certainty of being all reality" (142; 181), is left strangely abstract and one-dimensional, and cannot yet accede to genuine individuality insofar as it remains unconsciously locked into the mind of the individual scientist or observer, the individual practitioner of this abstract Reason. The moment of Reason here is therefore not yet the discovery of Spirit, but rather that of the emergence of *Vernunft* or Understanding (142, 144; 182, 184)—an essentially spatial and non-reflexive mode of consciousness.

With the self-consciousness chapters, and up to the emergence of Spirit as such, we traverse a seemingly heterogeneous mixture of subjects, which include chapters on the history of philosophy and the emergence of natural science, as well as brief but probing excurses into passion (hedonism, romanticism, and eighteenth-century virtue), along with the emergence of modern or secular individuality. In their various ways, all theses topics lay the groundwork for the more recognizably historical chapters of the section entitled "Spirit," which I have translated here as the social collectivity. A first pair of chapters ("Self-consciousness") lay in place a kind of existential progression, which includes the famous section on the struggle between Master and Slave, and the various existential-metaphysical options on offer in the desolation of the Roman Empire: stoicism, skepticism, and Christianity (the Unhappy Consciousness). The next or transitional group of chapters, entitled "Reason" (and posing the significant question of its possible distinction from self-consciousness on the one side and Spirit on the other), take up the topics of science (classificatory, psychological and as it were neuro-materialistic), libido, and work.

These are then the epistemological, psychoanalytic and Marxian preconditions not only for individualism and modernity, but above all for the full-blown emergence of History in the chapters organized around Spirit. For reasons to be discussed later on, I read the chapters on Spirit as the *Phenomenology*'s conclusion (its climax in the opposition between the revolution and Kantian morality), with the immense chapter on religion and the relatively perfunctory one on Absolute Spirit as textual supplements of one kind or another.

The same description may incidentally be applied to religion, whose recurrence in Self-consciousness ("the Unhappy Consciousness"), in Spirit ("belief and pure 'insight'"), and finally in a whole immense subsection (CC) entirely devoted to it, may otherwise be confusing. These returns, something like the progressive intersections of a single vector with the loops of a spiral, might better be grasped on the order of the musical theme and variations, as we will see later on. In any case, it is clear that the first-mentioned of these discussions of religion isolates the experience of an individual consciousness, the second one that of a significant social movement at a certain moment of history, and the third a whole social structure as such.

The Spirit chapters now unroll into what is a recognizable linear historical sequence, omitting, as I have already pointed out, the darkest Middle Ages (presumably on the ground that Christianity has already been dealt with). So we move directly from the polis and its vicissitudes (Antigone)—the ethical order—to the early modern and the emergence of the absolute monarchies from feudalism: this is now significantly entitled Culture, and prepares the way for the discussion of what we now call the public sphere in the eighteenth-century Enlightenment, with its dialectical struggle against religion or Christianity which has now sunk to the status of a "belief." There then follows the French Revolution and the Terror, to which I see the following chapter on Kantian morality in synchrony as a pendant, and which will for us be read, not as Kojève's end of history, so much as the suspended step of a present as much ours as Hegel's.

It would then be tempting to oppose the collective sense of Spirit to some individual perspective in the earlier chapters: but this is to presuppose that there could be any coherent individual perspective outside the collective existence in which individuals always find themselves. What could possibly be individual, in some existential sense, about the dialectic of sense-perception? That dialectic, to be sure, does involve some common-sense empiricist ideologies, which it undertakes to deconstruct; but one can hardly maintain that the operations of the individual senses and their objects absorb the totality of the individual existence (or at least one cannot do so until a certain modernism in art). The first three philosophical chapters are then truly technical, in the sense that they isolate specialized problems touching on this or that isolated feature of individual existence, and not, as is later the case with Spirit or with religion, the whole of it: but this is why these chapters, "moments" though they are (in that specific sense in which the German neuter noun "Moment" means an aspect, rather than, as with the masculine noun, a temporal phenomenon), designate levels of life which are always with us and whose very errors or commonplace stereotypes persist through all the "shapes" of history. Sense-perception is always with us, and in an historically far more significant way, so is the dialectic of the Master and the Slave: nothing excludes the latter's ongoing presence from the seemingly later chapters on the polis, absolutism, or revolutionary democracy. The same can no doubt be said for "observing Reason," the practice of a scientific investigation of nature and of both outside and inner worlds, as well as for the passions, the various ethics, and the religious anxieties. (Another weakness of the "post-Kantian" school may be conjectured here, in the way in which the more passional or ethical materials of the Reason chapter are relegated to "sociology" and thus implicitly dismissed as unworthy of technical philosophizing.)

On this view, then, it is not (it is no longer) a good idea to think of the *Phenomenology* as a kind of *Bildungsroman*, a form which, in a true Enlightenment spirit, tells the story of the progression of an immature subject to a state of maturity, very much in Kant's original sense: a "formation" or "education" brought about by the combined effects of inner dispositions and external experiences. The idea of maturation—autonomy, responsibility, self-government and the like—is certainly one of the most influential ways in which Hegel and his contemporaries conceptualized the bourgeois revolution (for which the notion of modernity is in any case a misnomer and an anachronism), living it as a fundamental historical break and as the central event of History at least since the Reformation; and it is clear from a juxtaposition of his revolutionary chapter ("Absolute Freedom and Terror") with the following one on morality that he saw Kant's ethics as a crucial contribution to the new post-revolutionary world, both as a sign of profound change and as an attempt to theorize and to resolve the new problems to which it gave rise. But it's not clear to me that this particular historical plateau is endowed with a vision of some new centered and fulfilled subjectivity (and to read Absolute Spirit in that way is to turn Hegel back into the caricature he has been for so many years).

Even less satisfactory is any attempt to make such a view of the subject (albeit immature and still in tutelage) retroactive to the initial chapters of the book which as we have seen at best pose aspects of the problem of consciousness, but not of any unified subjectivity. It would be tempting, then, to think of those early chapters in terms of split subjectivities, multiple subject-positions, part objects, semi-autonomous drives and the like; but that is surely even more anachronistic and without any persuasive evidence. If what is wanted is some line of narrative continuity—and the desire and its accompanying anxiety say as much about the reader as about the author's project—then at best the chapters are shadowed by sequences from the history of philosophy as Hegel saw it. In that case they project but local sequences scarcely bound by the rules of chronology, and which are in any case mostly assimilated to the illusions of common sense and the ideologies of everyday life. Thus the opening chapter on "sense certainty" posits a world in which the things we see and touch around us constitute reality as such and are self-evidently the worthiest of our trust.

Meanwhile, a more comprehensive kind of illusion slowly develops throughout these first chapters and which we must call, as though it were a specific faculty of the mind, *Verstand* or understanding: this is what we might now today call common sense: reified thinking, the thinking of the external, of space and objects generally, a thinking ultimately abstracted and codified in mathematics. The two *Logic*s undertake the most thoroughgoing demystification of this "faculty," which we tend to apply indiscriminately and illicitly to all kinds of other phenomena, such as thoughts and concepts, feelings, history, relations with other people, and so forth. I call this a faculty (a view inherited from Kant) because although it will come to be corrected by different kinds of thinking, it is obvious that it must remain the conceptual lingua franca of our everyday life in what it takes to be a material world. In typically dialectical fashion, it is an error, but an error that it would be disastrous to do away with, and that can only be sublated or *aufgehoben*: that is, it will continue to exist on the level appropriate to it, but now coordinated with some very different conceptual dynamics.

Before taking on any of this substantively we need to ponder a methodological issue and to forestall one of the most notorious and inveterate stereotypes of Hegel discussion, namely the thesis-antithesis-synthesis formula. It is certain that there are plenty of triads in Hegel, beginning with the Trinity (or ending with it?). It is also certain that he himself is complicitous in the propagation of this formula, and at least partly responsible for its vulgarization. It is certainly a useful teaching device as well as a convenient expository framework: and is thereby called upon to play its role in that trans-formation of Hegel's thought into a systematic philosophy—into Hegelianism, if you will—on which we will have occasion to insist over and over again in the present essay. For even if the tripartite rhythm happens to do justice to this or that local Hegelian insight, it still reifies that insight in advance and translates its language into purely systemic terms. (Indeed, for contemporary philosophy it is precisely this sequence which is identifiable as being teleologi-cal, so that today—or perhaps from Freud on—we tend to reverse this order and to affirm that it is the antithesis which produces the thesis in the first place, in order to generate the ideological illusion of the synthesis as such. It may be observed that the new version of causality performs the same operation on the old one.) Meanwhile, the tripartite formula is calculated to mislead and confuse the reader who seeks to process this material in a series of three steps: something for example utterly impossible to complete in the structurally far more complex play of oppositions in the chapter on the secular culture of absolutism; and alarmingly rebuked by Hegel himself in that famous passage at the end of the greater *Logic* in which he allows that "three" might be "four" after all.[13]

Yet the tripartite temptation does not appear out of nowhere, nor does it correspond to nothing at all. Indeed, it might be considered a relatively awkward codification of what is certainly a far more consistent and coherent Hegelian view of human time, which governs the growth of the individual (*Bildung*) fully as much as the development of history itself. This is the great rhythm of internalization and externalization in which Hegel both coincides with Marx and differentiates himself sharply from Marxism. For the various words Hegel uses about this process—*Entäußrung, Entfremdung*—all of them corresponding to the literal meaning of the word alienation—open that conceptual space in which Marx himself, adopting this systole and diastole of the production process, seeks to distinguish *alienation* from objectification or externalization in a way which will ground a properly Marxian view of history. Nonetheless we will see that Hegel's notion of work or activity, which is the source of the rhythm whereby we objectify ourselves and then reinteriorize the objective results at some higher level, is profoundly dialectical and is scarcely cancelled by the Marxian correction. It is all the more useful a concept for us today, as we shall see, in that it posits a rhythm of expansion more helpful in conceptualizing contemporary spatiality than it would have been in an earlier period. Finally, it is the source of some of Hegel's most significant and insistent linguistic figures, in particular the language of a "going back into" the self or consciousness, a trope far more important for the understanding of

---

[13] See Hegel, *Wissenschaft der Logik*, in *Werke*, vol. 6, 564; or *Hegel's Science of Logic*, trans. A. V. Miller, London: George Allen and Unwin, 1969, 836. I am indebted to Slavoj Žižek for drawing my attention to this interesting passage.

the Hegelian text than the standard tripartite language, whose final term, "synthesis," presupposes a resolution in this movement which is not at all consistent with Hegel's thinking; positing a kind of success or progress in externalization and internalization which scarcely does justice to Hegel's deeper appreciation of failure and contradiction and turns the historical movement of the dialectic into a banal and uplifting saga of inevitable progress.[14]

The tripartite scheme itself has a different origin, however, and it is to be located in one of the most inveterate figures of the Hegelian text, namely that which seeks to assimilate thinking and its temporalities to that amphibious thing, the proposition (*Satz* or sentence) in logic—a sentence which is also a judgment, and whose strongest and most unique form is reached in the syllogism.[15] The extraordinary productivity of this fascination of Hegel with logic reaches its fruition in the greater *Logic* of 1812–1816, in which, in a stunning and wholly unexpected resurrection, the whole dead weight of the scholastic elaboration of Aristotle's logical compendia is miraculously translated and transmuted into substantive dialectical categories. In the *Phenomenology* we only sense the first stirrings of this mighty project, and it is best to take them as figures rather than as ideas in their own right. Thus we will say that the syllogism is here little more than one crystallization among others of the specialized temporal cadences Hegel is here concerned to collect: the logical figures are one convenient way of transcribing and scoring such moments, with the advantage that this particular figure is also auto-referential, and that its own specific content—subject, predicate, affirmation, negation— can also serve as an interpretant of what we find here transpiring. (It is not until the third and final, "speculative," panel of the *Logic* that the syllogism bursts forth as the very embodiment of Life itself.) But

---

[14] "Does not Hegel's *Phenomenology of Spirit* tell us again and again the same story of the repeated failure of the subject's endeavor to realize his project in social substance, to impose his vision on the social universe—the story of how the big 'Other,' the social substance, again and again thwarts his project and turns it upside-down?" Slavoj Žižek, *The Ticklish Subject*, London: Verso, 1999, 76.

[15] See Günter Wohlfahrt, *Der Spekulative Satz*, Berlin: de Gruyter, 1981.

here, at this lower level, it is best to think of the logical episodes as yet more picture-thinking (Miller's welcome translation of *Vorstellung*).

The view of logic with which we then emerge is one in which attention and its thinking veers around under its own weight: the logical subject, of which a predicate is affirmed, now, insofar as it is at one with that particular predicate, loses its priority; the predicate, now becoming the substance itself, has shifted to the center of things, the former subject now reduced to little more than the predicate of that former predicate. It will be remembered that the young Marx took this whole process as the very paradigm of Hegel's profound idealism, which turns abstractions into things at the same time that it turns real things into abstractions.[16] What casts a somewhat different light on this suspicious procedure is its restlessness (one of Hegel's favorite words), which allows none of these developments to settle down in a stable place or being. Indeed, as Adorno has argued, when in doubt, Hegel (straining to restore content to the subjectivisms of Fichte and Schelling) always inclines in the direction of the "preponderance of the object." Thus, in characteristic micro-narrative, he conveys something of the frustration of the former "subject" of the proposition, which

> still finds in the Predicate what it thought it had finished with and got away from, and from which it hoped to return into itself; and, instead of being able to function as the determining agent in the movement of predication, arguing back and forth whether to attach this or that Predicate, it is still really occupied with the self of the content, having to remain associated with it, instead of being for itself. (58–59/37–38)

And now, unexpectedly, not only is "the general nature of the judgment or proposition . . . destroyed by the speculative proposition," but the whole figure is effaced by a new, musical one: "this conflict between the general form of a proposition and the unity of the Notion which destroys it is similar to conflict that occurs in

---

[16] Karl Marx, "Critique of Hegel's Doctrine of the State," in *Early Writings*, trans. R. Livingstone and G. Benton, London: Penguin, 1975.

rhythm between metre and accent" (59/38). This illustration will be enough to warn us against identifying Hegel's thinking with any of the figures he uses to describe it.

Some of them, to be sure, if properly marked as figures in advance, can be helpful in isolating this or that significant feature: the tripartite formula, for example, can suggest the all-important unity of opposites by way of its first two terms, and provided we abandon the obsessive search for syntheses. Meanwhile, the form of the syllogism can also be useful if we focus attention, not on its results or conclusions, but rather on that "middle term" shared by both subject and predicate—a kind of Hölderlinian primordial unity, from which, as we shall see, both terms emerge and to which they strain to return at the end of the logical process. Even these examples, however, suggest yet a further lesson, namely the need to stress an open-ended Hegel rather than the conventionally closed system which is projected by so many idle worries about Absolute Spirit, about totality, or about Hegel's allegedly teleological philosophy of history.

Indeed, the doctrine of the middle term suggests a very different Hegel who may serve as a corrective to the traditional ones: this is the Maoist Hegel proposed by Alain Badiou, in which the metaphysical spirit is expansive rather than centripetal or cyclical. Here the central dialectical movement is identified as the One dividing into Two, and it is clearly quite distinct in spirit from those figures that emphasize (for example) the return of consciousness into itself (350–351, 425).[17] We will also return to this new pattern of infinite scissiparity (which is to be found explicitly articulated in Hegel's political thought) later on.

For the moment, it is enough to conclude these initial remarks with the conviction that we must try in what follows to separate

---

[17] See Mao Tse-tung, "A Dialectical Approach to Inner-Party Unity," *Selected Works of Mao Tse-tung, Vol. V*, Peking: Foreign Language Press, 1977, 514-516; Guy Debord, *Society of the Spectacle*, Detroit: Black and Red, 1983, chap. 3; Alain Badiou, *Théorie du sujet*, Paris: Seuil, 1982, 61-62, 131, 228-229; and also the relevant chapter in (forthcoming, Bruno Bosteels, *Badiou and Politics*, Durham: Duke University Press). And see also Alenka Zupancic, *The Shortest Shadow: Nietzsche's Philosophy of the Two* (Cambridge: MIT, 2003).

the events of Hegel's text from the terms and figures in which they are presented. But this is easier said than done, for it involves the contradictory presupposition that the fundamental problem can be stated in non-representational terms, as though what we were calling "representation" were some mere decorative adjunct to what can also be presented neutrally or objectively. At that point, then, every effort to convey some original thought of Hegel before its expression in what he found to be a satisfactory formulation is itself in turn drawn back into the representational dilemma in a never-ending asymptotic spiral.

But the dilemma can perhaps better be conveyed in another figure, on which we have already touched. This is the musical phenomenon of the theme and variations, and it is surely no accident that the master of this musical figure is Hegel's exact contemporary. Indeed, it may even turn out that the compromises on which Beethoven himself (and the first Vienna school in general) founded their "classicism," also have some analogy with Hegel's own problems and solutions. Here is what Adorno has to say about Beethoven's practice of theme and variations and indeed its centrality in this whole moment of musical history:

> Development recalls the procedure of variation. In music before Beethoven—with very few exceptions—the procedure of variation was considered to be among the more superficial technical procedures, a mere masking of thematic material which otherwise retained its essential identity. Now, in association with development, variation serves the establishment of universal, concretely unschematic relationships. The procedure of variation becomes dynamically charged with newly gained dynamic qualities. In variation, as developed up to this point, the identity of the thematic material remains firmly established—Schoenberg calls this material the model. It is all "the same thing." But the meaning of this identity reveals itself as non-identity. The thematic material is of such a nature that to attempt to secure it is tantamount to varying it. It really does not in any way exist "in itself" but only in view of the possibility of the entirety. Fidelity to the demands of the theme signifies a constantly intervening alteration in all its given moments. By virtue of

such non-identity of identity music achieves a completely new relationship to the time within which a given work takes place. Music is no longer indifferent to time, since it no longer functions on the level of repetition in time, but rather on that of alteration. However, music does not simply surrender to time, because in its constant alteration it retains its thematic identity. The concept of the classic in music is defined by this paradoxical relationship to time.[18]

Adorno's discussion is not by chance embedded in his essay on Schoenberg, where it marks that possibility of a transgression of limits already foreshadowed in the limit itself. For as Adorno implies, the very notion of the theme is a fragile and precarious one, which will in Schoenberg's hands (and under what Adorno considers to be the objective logic of the musical material itself) give way. For the well-nigh infinite virtuosity of the variational process itself (we often indeed begin with a variation, and only later on discover the theme as such, in its official or "original" form) at length leads to a kind of musical "critique of origins," that is to say, to the nagging doubt as to whether there ever was such a thing as the initial theme in the first place. Yet if the theme itself also comes to be considered a variation, it then turns out, in truly postmodern fashion, to have been a variation without an original, much as present-day simulacra are described as copies without originals. We therefore here arrive at a decisive moment dialectically, in which difference, by gradually extending its dominion over everything, ultimately comes to liquidate identity as such, in a well-nigh suicidal meltdown in which it must itself also disappear (inasmuch as difference is necessarily predicated on identity in the first place).

The classical form of theme and variations is then secretly inhabited by this contradiction, this fateful inner tendency, which it can only provisionally and temporarily forestall by some initial act of faith in the stability and identity of the theme as such. It is a dilemma we may now retranslate into conceptual terms, where the term reification seems the

---

[18] T. W. Adorno, *Philosophy of Modern Music*, trans. Anne Mitchell and Wesley Blomster, New York: Seabury Press, 1973, 55–56.

most appropriate way to convey a linguistic parallel. The compromise belief in the stability and substantiality of what is in music called the theme is here in philosophy echoed in the mirage of the invention and defense of a correct language, that is to say, a set of stable names for the philosophical problems and their putative solutions. The systems of the traditional philosophers are then in effect constituted by systems of names, by a specific nomenclature, associated above all with the name of the philosopher (Lacan taught us that names and -isms were the very hallmark and symptom of so-called university discourse[19]). The stability of the names, and the prospect of widespread adoption and adherence to them, is a well-nigh religious mirage of universality whose destructiveness has come to be only too well-known, without there seeming to be any other alternative than the reformation-style pluralism of multiculturalist "interpretive communities."

The problem with names is that, deeply embedded in history, after a certain time and at different rates of speed they begin to show their age. Some systems are canonized and as it were mummified, others begin to rot and stink of an intolerable past, still others give off the musty smell of archives and long-shuttered houses. There then gradually arises a new kind of philosophical ambition, not merely to invent a foolproof new system of correct names, but also somehow to elude the ravages of temporality and to invent remedies to ward off the inevitable historical reification of these historical linguistic systems (the word "reification" is of course itself just another such historical name). The prestidigitation of an operation that might be called name and variations is only one attempt to move so fast as to elude the fatal process; another is the Magritte formula ("ceci n'est pas une pipe") in which, marked as names from the outset, the formula in question is already as it were homeopathically secured against some later denunciation. But of course all such operations are themselves the signals of their own historicity, and condemned, like past fashions, to go into the past without the kind of immortality they desperately sought.

---

[19] Jacques Lacan, *Le séminaire, livre XVII: L'envers de la psychanalyse*, Paris: Éditions de Seuil, 1991, 79–119.

One may argue that in the case of Hegel—as with Beethoven himself—while historicity cannot but be present, there remains a certain distance between the theme or the name and the musical or philosophical operation in such a way that they can be rewritten in the present with a certain effective afterlife, even though they cannot but remain dead. It would be tempting to call this distance the dialectic, were not this last a historical name like everything else, with its own museum waiting for it.

Chapter 3

Idealism

It is best to begin one's description of Hegel's conceptual operations with a specific methodological peculiarity which is associated with the period historical term "*setzen*" or "to posit." The term is probably an invention of Fichte's, or at least one brought into wider currency and foregrounded by him, insofar as his own philosophical system turned on the primal act whereby the subject or the I somehow "posits" the not-I in some first "big bang" theory of Being. But Hegel's wide-ranging use of the act of positing is scarcely so melodramatic as this and offers a better way of grasping the dialectical operation as such than all the triadic movements customarily associated with that process.

It would be tempting to describe what is posited in terms of presuppositions: for positing somehow always takes place "in advance" of other kinds of thinking and other kinds of acts and events, and the grasping of what has already been posited ("always-already," as one successful contemporary formula has it) is often taken to be the surest road to analysis and to understanding the structure of what happened "in the first place." Yet presuppositions and presupposing would seem to anchor us firmly in mental operations and in thinking as such: at best they could lead to ideological critique and to the unmasking and denunciation of prejudices: even there, however, Gadamer's denunciation of the prejudice of such ideas of "prejudice" is helpful,[20] insofar as it reminds us that what we are really interested

---

[20] Hans-Georg Gadamer, *Wahrheit und Methode*, Tübingen: JCB Mohr, 1960.

in is not thinking so much as being-in-the-world, and that while there can certainly be errors and unwarranted presuppositions in thinking, it is a little harder to imagine what form those might take existentially.

Thus, rather than thinking in terms of axioms, belief, presuppositions, and other such conceptual ballast, it might be better to try to convey the specificity of positing in terms of theatrical settings or pro-filmic arrangements, in which, ahead of time, a certain number of things are placed on stage, certain depths are calculated, and an optical center also carefully provided, the laws of perspective invoked in order to strengthen the illusion to be achieved. Even though the suggestion of fictionality and of calculated illusion remains very strong in this example, it might well help to convey the kind of analysis necessary to explain the effects of a spectacle provided in advance: how the sets were put together, what the lines of flight are, the illusion of specific depths, the lighting in foreground and background, etc.

The most famous exemplification of positing for the post-Kantian philosophers was indeed the one to which the above-mentioned act of Fichte attempted to respond and that is Kant's idea of a *noumenon* or thing-in-itself. The separation of reality into things as they appear to us and unknowable things-in-themselves is generally thought to be a compromise whereby Kant saves objective reality itself along with the development of a very refined and complex structural analysis of the ways in which the human mind necessarily processes the inaccessible raw data of that reality. Compromises, however, never really last (even though this one, like Aristotelianism before it, becomes for all its complexity the very working ideology of Western common sense); and Kant's solution, misunderstood as yet another idealism, albeit of a more complicated and subtle kind, satisfies neither the empiricists/realists on the one hand, nor the idealists on the other, that younger generation of post-Kantian German philosophers called into being by his extraordinary system. On the one hand it is felt that Kant's is essentially an analysis of what remain purely subjective projections out onto an unknowable world; while on the other, fault is found with the premise that there exists a kind of being about which, since by definition we cannot know it, it seems impossible that we should be entitled to affirm its existence in the first place.

Famously, Hegel's reaction to the sensible limits Kant's critique sets for human knowledge and philosophizing lies in a closer scrutiny of the very category of the limit itself: we cannot set a limit, he points out, without somehow already placing ourselves beyond that limit. It is a devastating insight, which at once destabilizes the *Critique* and deprives it of its carefully argued pre-philosophical (and anti-metaphysical) precautions: Hegel's post-Kantian colleagues already chafed at the ban on metaphysical speculation which the Kantian critique seemed to impose. Now, presumably, the floodgates have been opened.

But if Hegel's analysis of the limit characterizes a formal strategy for problematizing the doctrine of the noumenon, it does not seem to offer any particularly concrete way of dealing with the problem itself. This is then the function of the doctrine of positing or of the *setzen*: it will now transpire that Kant's theory—phenomenon and noumenon—looks somewhat different if it is grasped as a specific way of positing the world. At that point it is no longer a question of belief: of taking the existence of objective reality, of the noumenon, of a world independent of human perceptions, on faith. But it is also not a question of following in Fichte's footsteps and affirming that objective reality—the noumenon, which has now become the not-I—is summoned into being by the primal act of the I, which "posits" it (now using the term in a metaphysical sense).

Rather, that beyond as which the noumenon is characterized now becomes something like a category of thinking (along with the limit itself). It is the mind that posits *noumena* in the sense in which its experience of each phenomenon includes a beyond along with it; in the sense in which the mirror has a tain, or the wall an outside. The noumenon is not something separate from the phenomenon, but part and parcel of its essence; and it is within the mind that realities outside or beyond the mind are "posited." To be sure, the language of the mind and of thinking is too narrow and specialized for this more general structural principle, which is also a dialectical one. The more fundamental question for such a doctrine—or for such a method, for such a perspective, if you prefer—is not whether objective reality exists; but rather from what vantage point the operation of positing is itself observable. Are we not outside the mind in another way when we show how the mind itself posits its own limits and its own beyond? Are we not now obliged to appeal to some notion of reflexivity or self-consciousness in order to rise to such a new level, and is it not precisely that notion of reflexivity which is today everywhere philosophically called into question? I think this is so, and that we will need to return later on the vexed question of self-consciousness: we cannot deal with it now because we do not yet know where this new operation called positing (and its analysis and demonstration) will take us (to be sure, it will also take us all the way through the *Phenomenology* itself).

But we can at least perhaps now deal with the problem of idealism, which has not been disposed of by putting both Kant and Fichte in their respective places, and which indeed Hegel himself will seem to endorse with his slogan of "objective idealism," an attempt to square the circle which is unlikely to convince anyone. In any case Hegel continues to use the word idealism throughout in what may be seen as a fairly aggressive manner.

Take for example his pugnacious statement: "This ideality of the finite is the chief maxim of philosophy; and for that reason every genuine philosophy is idealism."[21] Yet the nature of this "ideality" remains to be identified. We make a beginning with the approach of *Verstand* to number: "Now number is undoubtedly a thought; it is the thought nearest the sensible, or, more precisely expressed, it is the thought of the sensible itself, if we take the sensible to mean what is many, and in reciprocal exclusion" (*EL*, 220; 154). This comment moves the scare-word idealistic much closer to what we call the theoretical, in the sense in which number is self-evidently a constituent

---

[21] G. W. F. Hegel, *Werke*, vol. 8, *Enzyklopädie der philosophischen Wissenschaften I: Wissenschaft der Logik*, Frankfurt: Suhrkamp, 1986, 203; in English, *Encyclopedia of Logic*, trans. William Wallace, Oxford: Clarendon Press, 1975, 140. Future references to this work are denoted *EL*; all page references will cite the German edition first, followed by the English translation.

part of a whole theoretical or structural system of number, rather than some ghostly underpinning of being itself, as the more programmatic positions of Pythagoras or Galileo might at first suggest. Idealism in this sense is not an ontological proposition at all, it is something closer to an epistemological one. Meanwhile Hegel's interesting qual-ification—that number is "the thought nearest the sensible," if not the latter's thought itself—will very much constitute the initial topic of the *Phenomenology*, whose opening chapter, on so-called "sense certainty," stages the paradoxical demonstration that what we grasp with our senses is not some unmixed immediate sensory reality, but is in fact, to put it indelicately, all mixed up with ideas and ideation. We will return to the demonstration in a moment.

But first it will be in order to offer a somewhat different under-standing of idealism than what is generally supposed when it is confused with spiritualism or thought to involve this or that ascetic repression of the body. It may well, to be sure, reinforce this last, as in Plato and to a certain extent Hegel himself—the arguments against the philosophical materialisms slipping insensibly into the expres-sion of a revulsion with the physical; but the two positions scarcely coincide, nor are they inseparable, as witness Spinoza's relationship with the body itself. We may also adduce the example of Berkeley's idealism, explicitly fashioned, he tells us, to restore an intensity of sensory perception deadened and muffled, philosophically obscured, by the various materialisms[22]: it is an argument—paradoxical for us today—which perhaps sheds new light on Bergson (and even on Deleuze). I should also here warn again against the assimilation of Hegel's technical term *Geist* to any of the various spiritualisms or religious philosophies. There is no reason to associate idealism with religion (or, I suppose, vice versa).

Idealism must be understood as a specific theoretical response to the peculiar problems of consciousness: indeed, materialism would in that case be understood first and foremost as a failure to pose those

---

[22] George Berkeley, *A Treatise Concerning the Principles of Human Knowledge*, in *The Works of George Berkeley*, eds. A. A. Luce and T. E. Jessop, London: Thomas Nelson, 1949, 42, 72–73.

problems (and for Berkeley as well as Hegel, the philosophical defect of materialism lies in the incoherence of its concept of "matter" as such). Kant organized this problem in the most striking and productive way when he classified consciousness (the subject or the "soul") as a noumenon and denied any possibility of knowing it in itself. Others have helpfully used physical analogies to reinforce the point: our minds, looking out of our eyes, cannot see themselves or grasp what lies behind them. To shift from these physical analogies to temporal ones, it becomes clearer that as we are always conscious— even in sleep or dreams, a kind of lower level of consciousness or what Leibniz might call sensitivity—we cannot by definition know what it is to lack that "attribute": what Hegel's contemporaries called the not-I is that which consciousness is conscious of as its other, and not any absence of consciousness itself, something inconceivable except as a kind of science-fictional picture-thinking, a kind of thought of otherness. But it is hard to understand how we could know something without knowing what its absence entails: and it may well be, as Colin McGinn argues, that consciousness is one of those philosophical problems which human beings are structurally unfit to solve; and that in that sense Kant's was the right position to take: that, although its existence is as certain as the Cartesian cogito, consciousness must also remain perpetually unknowable as a thing-in-itself.[23]

This is not necessarily the last word on the matter, however, as agnosticism would seem to be a resignation to defeat and a less productive outcome than other conceivable ones. Hegel's idealism is one of those, and simply means that whatever we think about will remain thought, whatever else it may be. This can be taken as an affirmation of the situatedness of all thinking (something that will later on, in Heidegger, be thematized as such); but it does not necessarily imply the spiritualist consequence that in that case all being is thought in the first place; only the more obvious implication that all thought about being or beings is still also thought (or consciousness).

---

[23] Colin McGinn, *The Mysterious Flame: Conscious Minds in a Material World*, New York: Basic Books, 1999.

But now we can return to our earlier discussion of "positing." What does this idealism, as I've just characterized it, involve in the way of positing? It is clear enough that materialism will involve the positing of a beyond which exists independently of my consciousness (and which thereby also remains within my consciousness at the same time that it oversteps it). If such materialism constitutes a metaphysical proposition about reality, how then could any idealism avoid being metaphysical in its turn? I take it that what Hegel means by speculative is precisely this way of marking the unavoidably metaphysical act of positing a "beyond" as metaphysical in its very structure, as a hypothetical leap beyond which we cannot go. This third or speculative moment in Hegel's system, in which the substance of the outside world is affirmed as somehow being the same as that of subjectivity, in which the logic of the syllogism is affirmed as somehow being the same as that of life as such, constitutes Hegel's acknowledgement of a different kind of limit, which it may be better to examine historically rather than philosophically.

Chapter 4

Language

The abrupt beginning of the *Phenomenology*, in the medias res of the body's sensory certainties, is in many ways the same as the equally abrupt beginning of the *Logic* in some absolute antithesis between Being and Nothingness (in which even more paradoxically the two are affirmed to be somehow "the same"). For everyone, bodily sense perception (leaving aside for the moment Hegel's careful distinction between sense-certainty and perception, to which we will return in a moment) is the very privileged content of the now, of the absolute temporal present in which we live at all times, and to that degree it is Being as such, before any distinctions between being and existence or any medieval or Heideggerian scruples about the difference between Being and beings. Sense is thus the primordial experience, which precedes all others if it is not prior to them, and to argue that it is somehow not as immediate and as privileged as it so obviously seems is a gesture as perverse as the unmasking of Being as Nothingness.

It is important to remember that consciousness is not at issue in this chapter, whose structure is thus very different from Descartes' opening move: the argument has little enough to do with consciousness and material being, indeed we scarcely even find a subject present here: with sense-certainty we have somehow preceded the very formation of subjecthood or of personal identity or personal consciousness. We are in a mythic state of the world, that "blooming, buzzing confusion" as which William James identified the body's awakening (or the world before philosophy); and it is this confusion that can loosely be characterized as *immediacy*, as a kind of deafening absence of negativities or distinctions. Not even individuality, the present, singularity, are words that can characterize this state, which precedes all the differentiations on which those concepts will later on be founded. Indeed, the only phenomenon which can in any way be structurally placed in relationship to this sensory plenitude turns out, in one of Hegel's most striking and original moves, to be language itself.

It is therefore necessary to say a word about Hegel's conception of language before proceeding; but in my opinion that word needs to be a negative rather than a positive one. Hegel certainly has a positive conception of language, most thoroughly formulated in his *Philosophy of Mind*, an *Encyclopedia* volume which is something like his anthropology and in which the nature and function of language is laid out very much in an Aristotelian spirit (Hegel was a great admirer of the *De Anima*). This "psychology" is the least interesting or original area of Hegelian thought, and has very little to do with the very striking appearances of language in the *Phenomenology*, where this alleged "faculty" is used in what it is not anachronistic to call a deconstructive way. The closest the dialectic comes to a productive discussion of language is to be found, unsurprisingly, in its view of the latter in terms of externalization and internalization; but little enough of the interesting surprises the dialectic so often reserves for us is to be found in this particular approach.

This is to say that, while language cannot be trusted to convey any adequate or positive account of the Notion, or of truth and reality—whence the tortured sentences and figures through which Hegel is forced to attempt such accounts—it can much more pertinently be used as an index of error or contradiction. Language, in other words, is more revealing for what it cannot say than it is for what it does manage to say: and this will clearly also mark the kinship of this moment of Hegel, not only with contemporary theory, but also with modernism in literature, where failure is so often more significant than success, and where the limits of language become the paradigm for the limits of representation as such.

But first we need to differentiate several distinct uses of language in this book, which are not necessarily unified by a concept. Language can indeed appear within a given historical moment (or "shape") as a component of that moment or an event within it: this is the case with the role of "counsel" in feudalism (307/374), the way in which the great barons serve emergent state power: already here, however, language is an ambiguous and often treacherous element, for as state power (the absolute monarch) becomes central, "the heroism of silent service becomes the heroism of flattery" (378/310), and the earlier useful speech turns into an empty name (the family name of the great nobles, reduced by Louis XIV to drones). Later on, as we proceed into the eighteenth century and the world of *Le neveu de Rameau*, flattery takes on a demonic appearance and acquires the power of an aggressive weapon, as the parasite Rameau recovers his centrality and his essentiality from his rich patron. But at this point language is still simply one element in a complex dialectic and has not "pervaded" (393/323) the whole.

Still, such historical contextualization is the moment for one of Hegel's more elaborate excurses, designed to anticipate the latter expansion and the more general identification of language with *Bildung* (translated "culture") to come. This is the discussion of language as alienation, *Entfremdung* (308/376), in a passage which anticipates most of Hegel's complex deployments of this unique phenomenon:

> But this alienation takes place solely in *language*, which here appears in its characteristic significance. In the world of ethical order, in *law* and *command*, and in the actual world, in *counsel* only, language has the *essence* for its content and is the form of that content; but here it has for its content the form itself, the form which language itself is, and is authoritative as *language*. It is the power of speech, as that which performs what has to be performed. For it is the *real existence* of the pure self as self; in speech, self-consciousness, *qua independent separate individuality*, comes as such into existence, so that it exists *for others*. Otherwise the "I," this *pure* "I," is non-existent, is not *there*; in every other expression it is immersed in a reality, and is in a shape from which it can withdraw

itself; it is reflected back into itself from its action, as well as from its physiognomic expression, and dissociates itself from such an imperfect existence, in which there is always at once too much as too little, letting it remain behind lifeless. Language, however, contains it in its purity, it alone expresses the "I," the "I" itself. This *real* existence of the "I" is, *qua* real existence, an objectivity which has in it the true nature of the "I." The "I" is this particular "I"—but equally the *universal* "I"; its manifesting is also at once the externalization and vanishing of *this* particular "I," and as a result the "I" remains in its universality. The "I" that utters itself is *heard* or *perceived*; it is an infection in which it has immediately passed into unity with those for whom it is a real existence, and is a universal self-consciousness. That it is *perceived* or *heard* means that its *real existence dies away*; this its otherness has been taken back into itself; and its real existence is just this: that as a self-conscious Now, as a real existence, it is *not* a real existence, and through this vanishing it *is* a real existence. (308–309)

Diese Entfremdung aber geschieht allein in der *Sprache*, welche hier in ihrer eigentümlichen Bedeutung auftritt.—In der Welt der Sittlichkeit *Gesetz* und *Befehl*, in der Welt der Wirklichkeit erst Rat, hat sie das *Wesen* zum Inhalte und ist dessen Form; hier aber erhält sie die Form, welche sie ist, selbst zum Inhalte und gilt als *Sprache*; es ist die Kraft des Sprechens als eines solchen, welche das ausführt, was auszuführen ist. Denn sie ist das *Dasein* des reinen Selbsts, als Selbsts; in ihr tritt die *für sich seiende Einzelheit* des Selbstbewußtseins als solche in die Existenz, so daß sie *für andere* ist. Ich als dieses *reine* Ich ist sonst nicht *da*; in jeder anderen Äußerung ist es in eine Wirklichkeit versenkt und in einer Gestalt, aus welcher es sich zurückziehen kann; es ist aus seiner Handlung wie aus seinem physiognomischen Ausdrucke in sich reflektiert und läßt solches unvollständige Dasein, worin immer ebensosehr zuviel als zuwenig ist, entseelt liegen. Die Sprache aber enthält es in seiner Reinheit, sie allein spricht *Ich* aus, es selbst. Dies sein *Dasein* ist als *Dasein* eine Gegenständlichkeit, welche seine wahre Natur an ihr hat. *Ich* ist *dieses* Ich—aber ebenso *allgemeines*; sein Erscheinen ist ebenso unmittelbar die Entäußerung und das Verschwinden *dieses* Ichs und dadurch sein Bleiben in seiner Allgemeinheit. *Ich*, das sich ausspricht, ist *vernommen*; es ist eine Ansteckung, worin es unmittelbar in die Einheit mit denen, für welche es da ist, übergegangen und allgemeines Selbstbewußtsein ist.—Daß es *vernommen* wird, darin ist sein *Dasein* selbst unmittelbar *verhallt*; dies sein Anderssein ist in sich zurückgenommen; und eben dies ist sein Dasein, als selbstbewußtes *Jetzt*, wie es da ist, nicht da zu sein und durch dies Verschwinden da zu sein. (376)

The passage at first seems to be a rehearsal, in the specific register or thematics of language itself, of that more general dialectic of externalization and internalization to which we have already briefly referred, but one which expresses itself through an opposition of form and content (unlike many of the other discussions of externalization as work or production). Here "counsel" begins as the content of this new secular post-sacred world of modernity as *Bildung* or culture: the barons impart wisdom and good sense to the king, they lay out the situation for him and point out the consequences good and bad—in other words, their language has determinate content and is worth what the content is worth. With the shift in gravity characteristic of the emergent absolute monarchy, little by little it becomes the form of language—the fact of speaking to the king, of having the right to speak to the king— which outweighs anything specific to be said to him. This shift is more than the mere status change of a language of equals into a language of courtiers, it is a foregrounding of language itself as such; nor is this a mere degradation of language's function. For what emerges in the increasing differentiation of language as a medium in its own right (and the function of that medium as message in the atmosphere of the court), is also paradoxically an emergence of individuality as such. The paradox is that my individuality, expressed through the first person of language, does not really come into existence until it exists "for others": we here discover a linguistic version of the dialectic of recognition that was hitherto visible only in the one-on-one hand-to-hand combat of the future master and the future slave.

This simultaneity of the coming into being of my individuality and its being-for-others—for which now the fateful word "universal" will be pronounced—is however itself the moment of a second unexpectedly complex and paradoxical dialectic: one in which the wordless unique individuality of my private "I" will vanish behind the public "I"—the shifter that belongs to everyone and that is the bearer of my recognition—a kenosis, as Hegel will call it, in which the private is emptied out in order to make way for the public.

Finally, we are given a glimpse of yet another peculiar development whose nature and consequences will only become apparent later on; and that is the characterization of this emergence of a public language, of what it is not premature to call the universal as well as the "public sphere," as an *Ansteckung*, an infection, something like the propagation of an odorless yet toxic gas through the atmosphere. We are perhaps still enough given over to the celebration of language and communication in the structuralist and poststructuralist period to be startled, if not shocked, by this unexpected figure, to which we will return (even though, from another perspective, it may be taken to anticipate a theory of the media).

Other seemingly secondary instances of language as an element within a moment are also liable to this kind of philosophical reversal and enlargement: thus Hegel's occasional reliance on colloquialisms—the telltale French epithet of "*espèce*" (drawn from *Rameau's Nephew*), or the untranslatable German expression "*die Sache selbst*" (the point, the main thing, the heart of the matter)—focuses their secret philosophical content like a burning glass. Meanwhile, reified phrases, alleged laws or ethical maxims, are relentlessly scrutinized until they become pointless tautologies ("differences which are no differences"); while in yet another dialectical reversal already discussed above, the most reified skeleton of language as such—the logical proposition or syllogism—suddenly proves to be the very vehicle for Life itself and the beating heart of the Notion or *Begriff*, the final stage of the Hegelian thought process.[24]

---

[24] Hegel's revival and transmogrification of the millenially mummified scholastic version of Aristotle's logic, his transformation of these dead forms back into genuine philosophical conceptuality, was of course his most intellectually original and audacious philosophical act.

We come at length to the most strategic use in the *Phenomenology* of language as diagnostic method, and that is what we have characterized as a properly Hegelian deconstruction; and this is scarcely limited to its most famous instance, the "disproof" of the certainty of sense-perception in Chapter 1. This striking demonstration can be seen as the radical incompatibility between the purest experiences of the body and its senses and the generalities of language as such: it is of course in some such way that modernism in the arts has waged a related campaign against the common-sense assumptions of representation.

But Hegel does not exactly interpret his own experiment in that way, contenting himself with observing that the accounts we give of sense-perception "do not say what they mean," do not say what they claim to say, or what they *mean* to say.

> Language, as we see, is more truthful; in it, we ourselves directly refute what we mean to say, and since the universal is the true [content] of sense-certainty and language expresses this true [content] alone, it is just not possible for us ever to say, or to express in words, a sensuous being that we mean . . . (60/85)

or, as he will add shortly, that we point at.

The kinship with deconstruction here is to be found not so much in simple failure or incapacity as rather in the way in which language sets an intention which it is constitutively incapable of keeping: in other words, it declares its own standard—what it means to say, indeed, what it is actually saying, its *vouloir-dire*, to use the Derridean phrase—and can therefore be measured internally by its failure to achieve the very standard it has set for itself and for which it has taken responsibility.

This is why the opening of the *Phenomenology* is much more than a mere gloss on "shifters," that is to say, on words such as "here," "now," and "I," which purport to render immediacy while being so empty of content as to house any momentary referent for which they are used: they cannot mean what they say. It is certainly a striking rehearsal of that phenomenon, but the reversal has a methodological afterlife at many other crucial points in the *Phenomenology*.

Thus the crucial phrase returns, even though it is here not yet a question of language, in the Master/Slave dialectic, in which it is observed that the "essential nature [of lordship] is the reverse of what it wants to be" (117/152); but the more powerful and satiric moments are those in which Hegel mocks the linguistic pretensions of empiricism on the one hand and "laws" of all kinds on the other: these represent the two equally futile poles of abstract reason—the attempt to turn the thinking about the observed outside world into a hard-and-fast fact and the attempt to formulate a generalization about the invisible processes alleged to stand behind the emergence of such observable "facts." "We see mere subjective imagining brought by the very nature of the fact to say—but *unthinkingly*—the opposite of what it affirms" (256/205): here the "fact" in question is truly a thing in all senses of the word, it is the skull bone itself, which phrenology affirms to be the same as thinking, just as the neuroscientists of our own time affirm the raw meat of the brain to be consciousness. (This particular "scientific" analysis give rise indeed to one of Hegel's most famous and scathing aphorisms: "spirit is a bone" [260/208]).

But the effort to formulate scientific laws is just as fraught linguistically, as we will have already learned in the chapter on "force." Indeed, as we shall see shortly, anything purporting to substitute possibility or potentiality for being, anything attempting to substitute a beyond for a here-and-now, is the object of the most vigilant Hegelian critique: and this is in a way the obverse of the critique of immediacy, for it attempts to undermine relationship in the opposite way, not by holding fast to the appearance, but by holding fast to the essence, to what lies "behind" and "within" phenomena. At any rate, such "laws" have their own dialectic: they purport to be reified or "*dingfest*" formulations, but must always be accompanied by voluminous explanations:

> Infinity, or this absolute unrest of pure self movement . . . first clearly and freely shows itself. Appearance, or the play of forces, already displays it, but it is as "explanation" that it first freely stands forth . . . The reason why "explaining" affords so much self-satisfaction is just because in it consciousness is, so to speak, communing directly with itself, enjoying

only itself; although it seems to be busy with something else, it is in fact occupied only with itself. (133–134/101).

But it is with moral laws that Hegel will be sterner in his pronouncements. For it is the ethical law of the "ought," the Kantian law of the *Sollen*—preeminently just such a substitution of possibility for actuality—which is the fundamental target of Hegel's commitment to immanence. "A whole nest of thoughtless contradictions" he names the moral worldview, which affirms itself as a moral agent by virtue of having to become one, and argues for the validity of ethical law at the same time that it certifies its non-observance in the real world (a non-observance which had justified the necessity of its own existence in the first place): two moments which are incompatible with each other and of which Hegel says: "because a moment has no reality for it, it posits that very same moment as real: or, what comes to the same thing, in order to assert one moment as possessing being in itself, it asserts the opposite as the one that possesses being in itself. In so doing it confesses that, as a matter of fact, it is in earnest with neither of them" (453–454/374). This "insincere shuffling," this "dissemblance," will then be denounced from one end of the chapter on morality to the other as "not taking the situation seriously" (454/375), "not being in earnest with moral action" (456/377).

But how can this be so, when we are dealing with so earnest a character as Kant himself, and what would it mean to take language itself seriously, when neither moralists nor scientists are able to do so? I think that their problem with language is two-fold: on the one hand none of them seems to realize that intention cannot be registered in language any more than sense-perception can. What they "mean," what they "want to say" or "intend," always fatally turns out to be the opposite of what they do say. They want language to express either the hard-and-fast fact or the beyond of appearance, while it can only convey the dialectical relationship between these opposites.

This is, indeed, then the other face of the problem: an attempt to use language in such a way that it short-circuits the unity of opposites and attempts to enact the law of non-contradiction within a medium that is preeminently one of a ceaseless movement back and forth between antitheses. Indeed, the prime "contradiction" of all speaking is one of the most fundamental manifestations of that "unity of opposites" rightly held to be the essence of dialectical thinking, and yet, as the matter of language itself makes clear, so difficult to realize in a practical speaking situation in which words get disambiguated whether they like it or not. Indeed, Hegel's own complex stylistic strategies show how complicated it is dialectically to show off the antithetical meanings latent in words and thoughts: for what often look like tortuous or inarticulate sentences prove to be carefully planned performances in the systematic changing of linguistic valences.

But this is only the most abstract way of characterizing the language problem in Hegel. The specific contradiction at stake here, from the first chapter onwards, is that between the individual speaker and the universality of language itself, and this is a tension which can scarcely be resolved. As we have seen, Hegel often dramatizes it as a sacrifice of the self, an emptying out (kenosis), an eclipse of individual subjectivity to the benefit of the universal of language. And to the degree to which Hegel understands his own position as a return to objectivity in the face of a rising tide of subjectivism (Jacobi, Schleiermacher, the Romantics, not to speak of the overestimation of the I in Fichte and Schelling), this surrender of the self no doubt often has a positive emphasis. Nor should we forget that universal here simply means other people, and that language is preeminently the medium in which other people are already present and precede our own individual appropriations, from childhood on. Language is thus already a symbolic apprenticeship of Spirit as a collective reality beyond the individual; and even personal or private expression necessarily takes place within an already established collective framework and as a reaction against it.

But this "preponderance towards the object," as Adorno called it, should not be distorted into some caricature of asceticism and renunciation: we will see later on that the great word *Befriedigung* or "satisfaction" (one of Kojève's favorite Hegelianisms) betokens a whole ethic that shares nothing with the ideals of duty in Kant let alone with the Platonic horror of the body (despite Hegel's "idealism"). Indeed, the *Phenomenology* does reach a moment of equilibrium between the individual and language's universalism; and to see it as the result of this tension which runs throughout the book itself is also better to understand the otherwise peculiar moment with which the *Phenomenology* ends (placing the narrative conclusion of the book before the Religion section as I will shortly explain), namely the seemingly ethical climax on confession and forgiveness. But these are in fact very precisely grasped as specific linguistic phenomena, and as structurally unique moments in which a subjectivity is able to universalize itself and to receive recognition or collective acknowledgement. Something of this "reconciliation" can already be glimpsed in the description of conscience that precedes a conclusion whose narrative significance we will discuss later on (480–1; 396–7).

> Whether the assurance of acting from a conviction of duty is *true*, whether what is done is actually a *duty*—these questions or doubts have no meaning when addressed to conscience. To ask whether the assurance is true would presuppose that the inner intention is different from the one put forward, i.e. that what the individual self wills can be separated from duty, from the will of the universal and pure consciousness; the latter would be put into words, but the former would be strictly the true motive of the action. But this distinction between the universal consciousness and the individual self is just what has been superseded, and the supersession of it *is* conscience. The self's immediate knowing that is certain of itself is law and duty. Its intention, through being its own intention, is what is right; all that is required is that it should know this, and should state its conviction that its knowing and willing are right. The declaration of this assurance in itself rids the form of its particularity, it thereby acknowledges the *necessary universality of the self.* In calling itself *conscience*, it calls itself pure knowledge of itself and pure abstract willing, i.e. it calls itself a universal knowing and willing which recognizes and acknowledges others, is the same as them—for they are just this pure self-knowing and willing—and which for that

reason is also recognized and acknowledged by *them*. In the will of the self that is certain of itself, in his knowledge that the self is essential being, lies the essence of what is right. Therefore, whoever says he acts in such and such a way from Conscience, speaks the truth, for his conscience is the self that knows and wills. But it is essential that he should *say* so, for this self must be at the same time the *universal* self. It is not universal in the *content* of the act, for this, on account of its specificity, is intrinsically an indifferent affair: it is in the form of the act that the universality lies. It is this form which is to be established as actual: it is the *self* which as such is actual in language, which declares itself to be the truth and just by so doing acknowledges all other selves and is acknowledged by them. (396–397)

Ob die Versicherung, aus Überzeugung von der Pflicht zu handeln, *wahr* ist, ob es *wirklich* die *Pflicht* ist, was getan wird,—diese Fragen oder Zweifel haben keinen Sinn gegen das Gewissen.—Bei jener Frage, ob die *Versicherung wahr* ist, würde vorausgesetzt, daß die innere Absicht von der vorgegebenen verschieden sei, d. h. daß das Wollen des einzelnen Selbsts sich von der Pflicht, von dem Willen des allgemeinen und reinen Bewußtseins trennen könne; der letztere wäre in die Rede gelegt, das erstere aber eigentlich die wahre Triebfeder der Handlung. Allein dieser Unterschied des allgemeinen Bewußtseins und des einzelnen Selbsts ist es eben, der sich aufgehoben [hat] und dessen Aufheben das Gewissen ist. Das unmittelbare Wissen des seiner gewissen Selbsts ist Gesetz und Pflicht; seine Absicht ist dadurch, daß sie seine Absicht ist, das Rechte; es wird nur erfordert, daß es dies wisse, und dies, daß es die Überzeugung davon, sein Wissen und Wollen sei das Rechte, sage. Das Aussprechen dieser Versicherung hebt an sich selbst die Form seiner Besonderheit auf; es anerkennt darin die *notwendige Allgemeinheit des Selbsts*; indem es sich *Gewissen* nennt, nennt es sich reines Sichselbstwissen und reines abstraktes Wollen, d. h. es nennt sich ein allgemeines Wissen und Wollen, das die anderen anerkennt, ihnen *gleich* ist, denn sie sind eben dies reine sich Wissen und Wollen, und das darum auch von ihnen anerkannt wird. In dem Wollen des seiner gewissen Selbsts, in diesem Wissen, daß das Selbst das Wesen ist, liegt das Wesen des Rechten.—Wer also sagt, er handle so aus Gewissen, der spricht wahr, denn sein Gewissen ist das wissende und wollende Selbst. Er muß dies aber wesentlich *sagen*, denn dies Selbst muß zugleich *allgemeines* Selbst sein. Dies ist es nicht in dem *Inhalt* der Handlung, denn dieser ist um seiner *Bestimmtheit* willen an sich gleichgültig; sondern die Allgemeinheit liegt in der Form derselben; diese Form ist es welche als wirklich zu setzen ist; sie ist das *Selbst*, das als solches in der Sprache wirklich ist, sich als das Wahre aussagt, eben darin alle Selbst anerkennt und von ihnen anerkannt wird. (480–481)

Chapter 5

Oppositions

The first three (technical-philosophical) chapters are however also an exposition and a laying in place of what may be thought to be (for Hegel) the great opposite number of dialectical thinking and that is the mode of thought called *Verstand* or understanding. As we have already seen, this is the thinking attributed to common sense: ordinary natural empirical thinking, of the type systematized in philosophy by Aristotle and later on (with a somewhat different dimension) by Kant, whose works are monuments to what may be called the working ideology of everyday life. As such, then, it is not so much a question of refuting this kind of thinking, without which none of us could live or function in what remains a Newtonian universe at the level of our bodily experience; as it is the drawing of boundaries and the designation of limits and insufficiencies. It is interesting to compare this philosophical program with Kant's, which was equally concerned to draw lines and to demarcate the claims of reason: but where Kant wished to suspend the illicit speculations about metaphysical areas (in which only belief is appropriate), Hegel, reinvigorating the pretensions of what he explicitly calls speculative thought, wishes systematically to unmask and to denounce the attempt to think the thought of reality in terms of what we may call spatial thinking, the thinking of externalities and of quantities.

For this kind of thinking—technically called *Verstand* or Understanding, following Kant's usage—is a thinking organized around the law of non-contradiction, a thinking for which only one pole of a given opposition or antithesis can be true at one time. But it is perhaps better not to approach Hegel's well-known dialectical "unity of opposites" in the mystical spirit it has so often seemed to express; better, perhaps, to begin to grasp its consequences in terms of that structuralism which, whatever its limits, had seemed for some, including myself, to signal a reawakening or a rediscovery of the dialectic. This would indeed be the moment to stage a generalized celebration of the binary opposition, as it freed us from the static substantialism of Aristotelian logic; and like so much contemporary philosophy, but in a far more strident and programmatic way, sought to promote relationality and the primacy of process and relativity—"differences without positive terms," as Saussure famously put it. Indeed, as we shall see, the most authentic way of grasping the dialectic will be the one able to think Hegel "without positive terms."

However this may be, it is certain that the *Phenomenology* is a profoundly structuralist work *avant la lettre*; and we could do worse than enumerate the various binary oppositions at work singly and in multiple combinations throughout these early chapters. We have already, in examining language, had to come to terms with that between the individual and the universal; but we have not insisted on the binary form that in fact regulates the play of those two terms, along with so many others in the later chapters, and that is the opposition between the essential and the inessential—what might today be called the center and the margin, or the dominant and the subordinate. Hegel's series of forms is unthinkable without the constant changing of places afforded by this formal alternation which is largely at one with what we have called positing. Thus, the "beyond" can be a secondary concomitant of perception and a way of organizing our relations with things; but it becomes essential in the religious conviction of its own inessentiality by the Unhappy Consciousness, in which the inaccessible "beyond" of God is posited as the essential.

With the chapter on perception, a new opposition enters the picture which was not particularly significant in the moment of sheer sense-perception (or "sense certainty") that preceded it; and that is the opposition between the one and the many, between unity and multiplicity. For just as a multiplicity of sensations slowly reorganizes itself into the individual thing and its many properties, so also something like a unity of consciousness appears out of the Deleuzian schizophrenia, the perpetual present, of the preceding moment of pure sensation. Indeed, it is this organizational primacy of the category of unity both in the object and the subject which will constitute Hegel's first evidence for that ultimate unity of subject and substances which he calls the speculative (and which is beyond all proof).

But the relative positions of these two opposites are not given in advance: we may well perceive the thing first and foremost as a unity, in which case it is either "(a) an indifferent, passive universality, and *Also* of many properties or rather 'matters'; or (b) negation, equally simply; or the *One*, which excludes opposite properties" (96/69). As the power of negation weakens, however, and the thing or object passes from the second of these emphases to the first, it becomes in the process a mere empty container for its many qualities or properties (form a), or in other words a third form, in which "the many properties themselves" are foregrounded and the thing becomes, in a memorable phrase, "the point of singular individuality in the medium of subsistence radiating forth into plurality"—"der Punkt der Einzelheit in dem Medium des Bestehens in die Vielheit ausstrahlend." But this is scarcely to be read as a standard tripartite movement, in so far as now the individual properties themselves enter into opposition with each other, giving rise to a new and ever more complex dialectic which will only be completed by the emergence of the beyond of "force" or "law" behind the thing and its properties alike.

This reemergence of the formal problem of the "beyond" will now be codified in a new opposition, namely that between expression and essence or law, in which the singular phenomenon to be explained, by virtue of being endowed with an explanatory law of which it becomes a mere example, sinks to the inessential symptom of a more essential yet imperceptible or invisible inner reality: a drift which then generates the more general category of appearance or *Schein* (sometimes awkwardly translated "show") which is successively invested and disinvested, not only with the opposition between inessential and essential, but also with that stronger version of the same opposition, which alternates between passivity and activity.

It is clear enough that such oppositions are designed to put order into this heterogeneous mass of data and to assign priorities such that scientific laws (of which causality is only one form) can be articulated and codified. But we must remember the satiric energy which the very concept of law calls forth in Hegel, and his passionately deconstructive repudiation of any naïve attempt to use language (very much including the "language" of mathematics) in this one-dimensional or affirmative way. The notion of law at once calls forth the dialectic of the beyond on the one hand and that of the *Sollen* or the ethical imperative, the appeal to mere possibility or potentiality, on the other.

The most famous Hegelian oppositions—positive and negative, identity and difference—are less to be regarded as the climax of this proliferation of binaries, than rather merely their strongest and most dramatic forms. Nor should we follow generations of Hegelian commentators in seeking to identify the ultimate forms in which such oppositions seem to be resolved (as though the greater *Logic* were itself simply moving towards some ultimate revelation). Rather, it is preferable to grasp each moment as an interminable play of oppositions without any stable resting places; and this is best done by scrutinizing those passages in which several oppositions play back and forth against each other in alternating pairs, such that content and form, essential and inessential, active and passive, are alternately superimposed on inside/outside, self and other, identity and difference, unity and plurality, and the like. This will train us in the exercise of a non-teleological Hegel, one whose fundamental polemic target is *Verstand* or empiricism: ideologies of non-contradiction which produce the mirage of an affirmative action as well as the reifications of a substantialist worldview. What happens when we try to reintroduce temporality or the form of History itself into this polemic remains to be seen.

Chapter 6

The Ethics of Activity (*die Sache Selbst*)

Before we do so, however, we must attempt to disengage and formulate something that must be called a Hegelian ethic. It is one of the centers of gravity of Hegel's philosophical thinking (they are multiple), and is certainly susceptible to systematization in the form of a codified and ultimately metaphysical system. Indeed, such provisional centers account for the way in which Hegel can be drawn in a number of incompatible ideological directions: this one left-wing and loosely Marxian, others (such as the alleged conservatism of his commitment to immanence) in some more right-wing direction. In fact, there are probably more possible Hegels available for ideologization than these two political opposites; but what needs to be reaffirmed at this point is the illicit nature of any such systematization, which amounts to the transformation of Hegel's thinking and his texts into that other thing called Hegelianism, a systematic philosophy and a metaphysics in whose construction he himself (particularly in the Berlin works) had no little complicity, but which as an ideology can be separated from the energy of his thought itself and the dialectic. Much the same operations can indeed be observed in the fortunes of Marx, whose writings Engels generalized into what has come to be called Marxism—a systematic philosophy which has several possible forms, an ideology with which one can certainly have some sympathy and even commitment (as I do), without seeking to conceal its radical distinction from what

I prefer to call Theory (or even theoretical writing), which makes no such systematic or philosophical claims.

Still, the Hegelian ethic I now wish to present is best grasped in the form of a kind of philosophy—if not the philosophy of praxis exactly, then at least the philosophy of production: the philosophy of Goethean *Tätigkeit* (or activity), of work, of externalization ("ubrigens ist mir alles verhasst, was mich bloss belehrt, ohne meine Tätigkeit zu vermehren oder unmittelbar zu beleben" [Goethe to Schiller, December 19, 1798]). It does not make its appearance in the *Phenomenology* until the celebrated Master/Slave chapter: a tardiness which itself casts an interesting light back on the emergent scientific theorization of "force" that preceded it (and that finds its fullest development in the more static pursuits of "observing reason" that follow).

For the upshot of the struggle between Master- and Slave-to-be is not at all the fulfillment of Desire: the latter is a good deal easier to deal with, as Hegel shows in a passage which vindicates Brecht's judgment of him as a great comic writer:

> With this appeal to universal experience we may be permitted to antici-
> pate how the case stands in the practical sphere. In this respect we can
> tell those who assert the truth and certainty of the reality of sense-objects
> that they should go back to the most elementary school of wisdom, viz.
> the ancient Eleusinian Mysteries of Ceres and Bacchus, and that they
> have still to learn the secret meaning of the eating of bread and the drink-
> ing of wine. For he who is initiated into these Mysteries not only comes
> to doubt the being of sensuous things, but to despair of it; in part he
> brings about the nothingness of such things himself in his dealings with
> them, and in part he sees them reduce themselves to nothingness. Even
> the animals are not shut out from this wisdom but, on the contrary, show
> themselves to be most profoundly initiated into it; for they do not just
> stand idly in front of sensuous things as if these possessed intrinsic being,
> but, despairing of their reality, and completely assured of their nothing-
> ness, they fall to without ceremony and eat them up. And all Nature, like
> the animals, celebrates these open Mysteries which teach the truth about
> sensuous things. (65)

Bei dieser Berufung auf die allgemeine Erfahrung kann es erlaubt sein, die Rücksicht auf das Praktische zu antizipieren. In dieser Rücksicht kann denjenigen, weiche jene Wahrheit und Gewißheit der Realität der sinnlichen Gegenstände behaupten, gesagt werden, daß sie in die unterste Schule der Weisheit, nämlich in die alten Eleusinischen Mysterien der Ceres und des Bacchus zurückzuweisen sind und das Geheimnis des Essens des Brotes und des Trinkens des Weines erst zu lernen haben; denn der in diese Geheimnisse Eingeweihte gelangt nicht nur zum Zweifel an dem Sein der sinnlichen Dinge, sondern zur Verzweiflung an ihm und vollbringt in ihnen teils selbst ihre Nichtigkeit, teils sieht er sie vollbringen. Auch die Tiere sind nicht von dieser Weisheit ausgeschlossen, sondern erweisen sich vielmehr, am tiefsten in sie eingeweiht zu sein; denn sie bleiben nicht vor den sinnlichen Dingen als an sich seienden stehen, sondern verzweifelnd an dieser Realität und in der völligen Gewißheit ihrer Nichtigkeit langen sie ohne weiteres zu und zehren sie auf; und die ganze Natur feiert wie sie diese offenbaren Mysterien, welche es lehren, was die Wahrheit der sinnlichen Dinge ist. (91)

The desire evoked in the self-consciousness chapter is a good deal more complicated than this one, and does not admit of any immediate physical satisfaction: Hegel seems to have cast an earlier version of this dialectic in sexual terms as a gender opposition[25]: and only later to have repositioned the sexual dialectic in the later chapters on "pleasure and necessity," "the law of the heart," and "virtue," and to have recast this one in the very different spirit of a desire for *recognition*, a conceptual innovation which has resonated down to the present day. It is clear that the thematics of recognition as such will have fundamental consequences for any politics, and that it will be more

---

[25] The two earliest versions of the Master/Slave dialectic both seem to have been elaborated in the Jena lectures (the so-called *Realphilosophie*) of 1802–1804 and 1805–1806. They are translated respectively as *System of Ethical Life*, eds. H. S. Harris and T. M. Knox, Albany: State University of New York Press, 1979, 238–40; and *Hegel and the Human Spirit*, ed. L. Rauch, Detroit, MI: Wayne State University Press, 1983, 191–193.

congenial for the politics of race, gender, and ethnicity than for class struggle.[26]

But this is not our topic for the moment, which has rather to do with the consequences of this recognition for the body and for production and consumption. The structure of this, the most famous chapter in the *Phenomenology*, is well known and has given rise to innumerable interpretative traditions. It was Alexandre Kojève whose commentary on the so-called struggle between the Master and the Slave (*Herr* and *Knecht*, more literally, the Lord and the Serf or Bondsman) placed this episode on the phenomenological as well as the political agenda. This is surely the first time in the history of philosophy in which the problem of the Other is thematized as such: reflections on solipsism and Descartes' musings about automata are by this decisive intervention at once transformed into dead ends and false problems. One line of filiation leads directly (without passing through Heidegger's notion of the *Mitsein* or "being with others," thereby itself revealed as yet another dead end) to Sartre's doctrine of the Look, which posits all individual relations as irresolvable conflict. The transformation of these individual confrontations with the Other into collective ones will then open this initial problem up to the theoretical innovations of the *Critique of Dialectical Reason*.

Meanwhile, Hegel's own thematization of the problem, along with its inevitable containment and reduction by way of the notion of "intersubjectivity," will give rise to a second—dare one say bourgeois?—philosophical and political tradition. Here the tradition of political "tolerance" and class or multicultural harmony denounced by Sartre becomes a political strategy of recognition, most notably theorized by Axel Honneth and, in a different way, by Jacques Rancière. We will evaluate these political prolongations later on when we return to Kojève.

---

[26] On the current "politics of recognition," it is best to begin with Axel Honneth, *The Struggle for Recognition*, trans. Joel Anderson, Cambridge: MIT Press, 1996; and Alexander García Düttmann, *Between Cultures*, London: Verso, 2000. The theme, indeed, reveals yet a third Hegel, alongside the Marxist and the fascist one, namely a "democratic" or Habermasian Hegel.

Yet the dialectical subtlety of Hegel's phenomenological analysis deserves its acknowledgement here. In a sense the struggle for mastery constitutes an externalization of the Unhappy Consciousness: where the latter posited an inward location in which my own self or consciousness—positioned as inessential, as contingent and worthless, as "unjustified," to use a later Sartrean language—confronts the absent yet essential and central transcendence it has itself posited. The Master/Slave struggle then exteriorizes both poles of this dialectical confrontation, whose outcome alone will determine to which side the qualifications of essential and inessential are to be applied. (Or rather, it would be more accurate to say that self-consciousness is only achieved by way of such externalization, and that the individual achievement of self-consciousness or reflexivity is itself dependent on some prior eruption of the Other into my field of experience.)

More significant than the external status and property categories are then these dialectical ones of essentiality and centrality, in terms of which the accession of the one anonymous consciousness to feudal lordship and domination is expressed, while the surrender of the other to what is his subaltern status *avant la lettre* will condemn him to serfdom or slavery (depending on the social paradigm in which we articulate this myth, so qualified because it is neither an historical event nor any permanent structure of human relationships). The stakes of this life-and-death struggle are not however, for Hegel, the will to domination and the drive for social power, but rather the necessity of recognition by the Other which Hegel attributes to the emergence of self-consciousness (and whose Sartrean version testifies that it need not be grasped in any edifying and pedagogical or developmental fashion).

As for the outcome, this brings us back to life and the body in a different way. For the master-to-be achieves his victory through his disdain for life (or perhaps we should say his indifference to his own death): recognition for him is the stubborn fidelity to honor, as one finds it in its various cultural avatars in aristocracies from medieval Europe to feudal Japan. The future slave, however, is committed to life and to the life of his own body under whatever conditions, preferring to submit rather than to die in the service of abstract value.

This would seem to place the Master in a more positive or philosophical light as some Hegelian or Platonic idealist, while the Slave—the Brechtian coward—is a materialist in his fear of physical death. Yet Hegel's discussion here takes a strikingly existential and even Heideggerian turn, as he celebrates the death anxiety and the capitulation of the loser to "the absolute Master, death." Here, indeed, *Angst* foreshadows what will later on be identified intellectually as absolute skepticism and then politically as absolute freedom (the Terror in the French Revolution), that is to say, as the supreme power and exercise of the Negative that breaks up and dissolves everything substantial in its path, everything subsisting in the status quo of ontic being as such:

> denn alles, was entsteht,
> ist wert, dass es zugrunde geht.
> *(Faust I)*

And the source for the coming-to-be of individual things is that into which destruction, too happens; for they pay penalty and retribution to each other for their injustice according to the assessment of Time. (Anaximander)

It therefore becomes less clear that it is the Master, who, rising above the body and its satisfactions, holds the place of wisdom; here, rather, the value of negativity trumps idealism and constitutes a philosophically more satisfactory force of the dissolution of the physical (and of everything else) than the Master's ignorant Samurai-like fearlessness.

This reversal is however already at the very heart of the dialectic of recognition itself: for each party gets what he deserves, and the victory of the Master is rewarded by his recognition as the very embodiment of the truly human by that sub-human loser who has become his slave.

The truth [of the master] is accordingly the servile consciousness of the bondsman ... just as lordship showed that its essential nature is the reverse of what it wants to be, so too servitude in its consummation will really turn into the opposite of what it immediately is; as a consciousness forced back into itself, it will withdraw into itself and be transformed into a truly independent consciousness. (152/117)

The exchange is however an asymmetrical one, and it is not quite accurate to say that the Master is thereby the truth of the Slave, for the Master has become a mere drone, for whom the Slave labors and whom he provides with the luxuries and necessities of life; the Master's aristocratic status consisting in his own professional duty, namely from time to time to wager his life in armed struggles of whatever kind.

The Slave's truth is thereby labor itself; his fearful preservation of the body and the physical has become a condemnation to perpetual labor on matter itself. At which point the Negative is itself clarified: and this *determinate* Negation of matter, which produces specific works and physical objects, is sharply distinguished from the absolute Negation which produces only death and destruction. It is at this point that we greet the first of Hegel's great celebrations of work:

> Through work, however, the bondsman becomes conscious of what he truly is. In the moment which corresponds to desire in the lord's consciousness, it did seem that the aspect of unessential relation to the thing fell to the lot of the bondsman, since in that relation the thing retained its independence. Desire has reserved to itself the pure negating of the object and thereby its unalloyed feeling of self. But that is the reason why this satisfaction is itself only a fleeting one, for it lacks the side of objectivity and permanence. Work, on the other hand, is desire held in check, fleetingness staved off; in other words, work shapes the thing. The negative relation to the object becomes its *form* and something *permanent*, because it is precisely for the worker that the object has independence. This *negative* middle term or the formative *activity* is at the same time the individuality or pure being-for-self of consciousness which now, in the work outside of it, acquires an element of permanence; it is in this way, therefore, that consciousness, *qua* worker, comes to see in the independent being [of the object] its *own* independence. (118)

Durch die Arbeit kommt es aber zu sich selbst. In dem Momente, welches der Begierde im Bewußtsein des Herrn entspricht, schien dem dienenden Bewußtsein zwar die Seite der unwesentlichen Beziehung auf das Ding zugefallen zu sein, indem das Ding darin seine Selbständigkeit behält. Die Begierde hat sich das reine Negieren des Gegenstandes und dadurch das unvermischte Selbstgefühl vorbehalten. Diese Befriedigung ist aber deswegen selbst nur ein Verschwinden, denn es fehlt ihr die *gegenständliche* Seite oder das *Bestehen.* Die Arbeit hingegen ist *gehemmte* Begierde, *aufgehaltenes* Verschwinden, oder sie *bildet.* Die negative Beziehung auf den Gegenstand wird zur *Form* desselben und zu einem *Bleibenden,* weil eben dem Arbeitenden der Gegenstand Selbständigkeit hat. Diese *negative* Mitte oder das formierende *Tun* ist zugleich *die Einzelheit* oder das reine Fürsichsein des Bewußtseins, welches nun in der Arbeit außer es in das Element des Bleibens tritt; das arbeitende Bewußtsein kommt also hierdurch zur Anschauung des selbständigen Seins *als seiner selbst.* (153–154)

Delayed gratification is certainly a notion familiar to us at least since Weber's *Protestant Ethic,* where, in the form of wages, it characterizes the cultural revolution specific to capitalism, the reorganization of the psyche required for the transformation of peasants into paid laborers. The new temporality Hegel has in mind here would seem rather to reflect the rhythms of handicraft production, insofar as the artisan is still able to recognize himself in the thing produced, in the matter thereby formed.

It is an impression that will be corroborated when we come to the full-dress celebration of work to be found in the great central chapter on "the actualization of rational self-consciousness through its own activity" ("die Verwirklichung des vernünftigen Selbstbewusstseins durch sich selbst" [section V-B]), followed up by that devoted to the ironically named "human zoology" or the so-called "spiritual animal kingdom" ("das geistige Tierreich" [section V-C-a]) and its conceptual centerpiece, the untranslatable "Sache selbst."

What is "die Sache selbst"? If you have to ask, then you may never know. I like to quote in this respect the most Hegelian moment in Thomas Mann's *Doktor Faustus*, in which the humanistic narrator asks his young friend Leverkühn, about to embark on a musical career, whether he knows of any feeling stronger than love: "Ja," replies Adrian coolly, "das Interesse." Interest indeed is in that sense the moment in which our productive being is virtually at one with that segment of the world immediately before it, in a kind of humble material enactment of the loftiest philosophical image of Absolute Spirit and the latter's hypothetical union between subject and object, Spirit and Nature. But Absolute Spirit is deliberately characterized as the climax of philosophy's third or speculative dimension (the other two are, depending on how you organize the work, *Verstand* and *Vernunft*—understanding and reason—or individual consciousness and Spirit—or even, following the *Logic*, being and essence).

Die Sache selbst, however—whether you translate it as "the matter at hand" or "the main issue," "the point," or "the heart of the matter"—is not a speculative possibility but a daily experience of what it might be better not to call the loss of self in activity, but rather its externalization. For this is, if anywhere, the moment in which some properly Hegelian ethic offers its most plausible chance to metaphysical and philosophical systematization. What can usefully block this temptation, however, is that complication of a single line of thematic opposition by the counterpoint of another one or even of several distinct binaries.

Thus here the alternation of externalization and exteriorization (a moment at the very end of the *Phenomenology* to be projected out— as *Erinnerung* [remembrance]—into a whole injunction to include history) is to be sure a familiar and even an inevitable one; but at this first moment of individuality (in Deleuze's language, "subject-ification") it is rhythmically combined with a tension between the particular and the universal, whose movement Hegel perhaps over-hastily dramatizes as a "sacrifice" (265; 213): a characterization he will immediately correct by adding that what is thereby "sacrificed"—"the need which the individual has as a natural creature [Naturwesen]" are in fact "not frustrated, but enjoy an actual existence" (265; 213) (the German—"Wirklichkeit haben"—is stronger than this English rendering, which only the emphasis on the Hegelian art-term "actuality" can properly convey). For it is the universal dimension of the process which alone turns "particularity" into "individuality" in the first place. The question then arises as to the nature and origin of this particular universality, which is clearly not that of language discussed earlier. What can translate the mindless individual effort of the body—as for example in the unloading of sacks of grain or the laborious opening of veins of coal in a mineshaft, the harvesting of potatoes or the nailing together of the planks of ship or house—into universality?

Here Hegel's simultaneous play of multiple oppositions may well seem prematurely to anticipate each other, and to stumble over their own rhythms. We have already hinted, and will explain later on in greater detail, that Spirit for Hegel—the eponymous *Geist* of this book—always means the collectivity, including custom as such (the "*Sitten*" of that word "*Sittlichkeit*" which is in Hegel to be translated as ethical substance rather than mere individual morality); indeed the recognition and resultant self-consciousness that already frames this chapter is already here characterized as a *Begriff* or notion that "includes the ethical realm" within itself (265; 212). It should then come as no surprise (but it does) that the discussion then suddenly celebrates the Nation—"the life of a free people," the "power of the entire people"—as that will form the climax of Goethe's *Faust II* some twenty-five years later, presumably as an alternative to the nationalist movement as well as to the Holy Alliance, in other words as a German appropriation of the republican spirit of the French Revolution.

But how this political presupposition of "the universal" is to be understood we will not clearly grasp until the later discussion of the "spiritual animal kingdom." For the French Revolution was not only an immense political overturning—the end of the feudal system on the night of August 4, 1789—the displacement of a whole aristocratic elite and of the monarchy itself by the masses of the common people—it was also the climax of a process of secularization as such. This process is not merely to be characterized as the coming of wage labor, although it was also that, but also as the liberation of human activity from the shackles of the sacred—the so-called "*carrière ouverte aux talents*": not just the possibility of rising beyond the traditional caste barriers of the old regime, but the plebeianization of that old religious conception of vocation as such or "calling": the chance now to follow one's interests and to practice whatever activity speaks to our individual subjectivities: a new freedom from the inherited métier of one's fathers and from the customary assignments of clan or village.

But this is now a peculiar enigma or mystery: how is it that I should be tempted by woodworking rather than by the forging of metals? And is my destiny as a weaver or a cobbler (the first political intellectuals) somehow inscribed in my being and the being of things and materials? Now the question is no longer "*comment peut-on être persan?*" but why one would wish to become a dentist or a cooper. The question no sooner poses itself than it is once again obscured and occulted by the forces of chance, money and family history; but Hegel continues to pose it with well-nigh ontological force, as his answer—the concept of the "spiritual animal kingdom"—testifies. For it is as though, like the species of natural beings, socialized humanity were also divided up into the innumerable species of the trades and the handicrafts, according to those "*Gaben und Fähigkeiten*"—"gifts and capacities"—whose notion emerges at this selfsame historical moment, and of which only that of genius tenaciously survives today (an idea which Kant theorized as a force of nature still persisting within us).

After a brief existential interlude, in which this new-found individuality explores its enjoyment of self in sexuality, the love-passion and the dialectic of virtue and mundanity—the references here are clearly Rousseau, Molière's *Le misanthrope*, and the general eighteenth-century preoccupation with virtue from Richardson to Sade and Robespierre—the concept of work returns, enlarged, as the very concept of action itself (the modern political theorization of *praxis* awaits Count Cieszkowski's essay of 1839), which is, I think, in Hegel primarily grasped as a form of *Tätigkeit*, that creative and productive activity which Goethe tirelessly practiced and celebrated.

Nor should it be expected that the pausing of the dialectic's inter-rogation on this form would leave it intact as some kind of natural unity: in Hegel, on the contrary, the act or action also dialectically "divides itself" into end, means, and result or object, and threatens to leave us with the disillusionment of intentions on the one hand and the sorriest unintended consequences on the other, if not the inability to begin in the first place, inasmuch as the work can never realize those initial dreams we may have had of it, leaving us either in the paralysis of indecision or the mechanical rote-work of repetition without ambition.

Such a stalemate is however always desirable in Hegel, for it calls forth all the energies of what we may now call his worldview.

Accordingly, an individual cannot know what he [really] is until he has made himself a reality through action. However, this seems to imply that he cannot determine the *End* of his action until he has carried it out; but at the same time, since he is a *conscious* individual, he must have the action in front of him beforehand as *entirely his own*, i.e. as an *End*. The individual who is going to act seems, therefore, to find himself in a circle in which each moment already presupposes the other, and thus he seems unable to find a beginning, because he only gets to know his original nature, which must be his End, *from the deed*, while, in order to act, he must have that End beforehand. But for that very reason he has to start immediately, and, whatever the circumstances, without further scruples about beginning, means, or End, proceed to action; for his essence and *intrinsic* nature is beginning, means, and End, all in one. As *beginning*, this nature is present in the circumstances of the action; and the interest which the individual finds in something is the answer already given to the question, "whether he should act, and what should be done in a given case." For what seems to be a *given* reality is in itself his own original nature, which has merely the illusory appearance of an [objective] being—an appearance implied in the Notion of action with its twofold aspect, but which shows itself to be his own original nature by the interest he takes in it. Similarly, the "how" or the means is determined in and for itself. *Talent* is likewise nothing else but the determinate, original individuality considered as an *inner means*, or as a transition from End to an achieved reality. But the *actual* means and the real transition are the unity of talent with the nature of the matter in hand, present in that interest: talent represents in the means the side of action, interest the side of content; both are individuality itself, as an interfusion of being and action. What we have, therefore, is a set of given *circumstances* which are *in themselves* the individual's own original nature; next, the interest which treats them as *its own* or as its End; and finally, the union [of these] and the abolition of the antithesis in the *means*. (240)

Das Individuum kann daher nicht wissen, was es ist, ehe es sich durch das Tun zur Wirklichkeit gebracht hat.—Es scheint aber hiermit den *Zweck* seines Tuns nicht bestimmen zu können, ehe es getan hat; aber zugleich muß es, indem es Bewußtsein ist, die Handlung vorher als die *ganz seinige* d. h. als *Zweck* vor sich haben. Das ans Handeln gehende Individuum scheint sich also in einem Kreise zu befinden, worin jedes Moment das andere schon voraussetzt, und hiermit keinen Anfang finden zu können, weil es sein ursprüngliches Wesen, das sein Zweck sein muß, *erst aus der Tat* kennenlernt, aber, um zu tun, *vorher den Zweck* haben muß. Ebendarum aber hat es *unmittelbar* anzufangen und, unter welchen Umständen es sei, ohne weiteres Bedenken um *Anfang, Mittel* und *Ende* zur Tätigkeit zu schreiten; denn sein Wesen und *ansich*seiende Natur ist alles in einem, Anfang, Mittel und Ende. Als *Anfang* ist sie in den Umständen des Handelns vorhanden, und das *Interesse,* welches das Individuum an etwas findet, ist die schon gegebene Antwort auf die Frage: ob und was hier zu tun ist. Denn was eine vorgefundene Wirklichkeit zu sein scheint, ist an sich seine ursprüngliche Natur, welche nur den Schein eines *Seins* hat—einen Schein, der in dem Begriffe des sich entzweienden Tuns liegt, aber als *seine* ursprüngliche Natur sich in dem *Interesse,* das es an ihr findet, ausspricht.—Ebenso ist das *Wie* oder die *Mittel* an und für sich bestimmt. Das *Talent* ist gleichfalls nichts anderes als die bestimmte ursprüngliche Individualität betrachtet als *inneres Mittel* oder *Übergang* des Zwecks zur Wirklichkeit. Das *wirkliche* Mittel aber und der reale Übergang ist die Einheit des Talents und der im Interesse vorhandenen Natur der Sache; jenes stellt am Mittel die Seite des Tuns, dieses die Seite des Inhalts vor, beide sind die Individualität selbst, als Durchdringung des Seins und des Tuns. (297)

This outburst is accompanied by a truly Sartrean repudiation of "exaltation, lamentation, or repentance" (297/240), without any attempt to disguise the alienation of the act into

> the antithesis of willing and achieving, between end and means, and again, between this inner nature in its entirety and reality itself, an antithesis which in general includes within it the contingency of its action . . .[the unity and necessity of the act] overlaps the former, and the experience of the contingency of the action is itself only a contingent experience . . . on the contrary, the antithesis and the negativity manifested in work affect not merely the content of the work *or* the content of consciousness as well, but affect the reality as such, and hence affect the antithesis present in that reality, and present only in virtue of it, and the vanishing of the work. In this way, then, consciousness is reflected out of its perishable work into itself, and preserves its Notion and its certainty as what objectively exists and endures in fact of the contingency of action. (302–304/246)

This exultation of the "thing itself" is explained by the "becoming conscious of this unity of its own actuality with the objective being of the world . . . since this unity means happiness, the individual is sent out into the world by his own spirit to seek his happiness" (268; 215). "The individual, therefore, knowing that in his actual world he can find nothing else but its unity with himself, or only the certainty of himself in the truth of that world, can experience only joy in himself" (299–300/242). But we will not fully appreciate the emotion of such passages—which also dramatize that Hegelian notion of satisfaction or fulfillment so dear to Kojève—without returning for a moment to contrast them with the more purely intellectual delight which Hegel attributes to abstract Reason's observation of the infinite variety of the natural world itself.

> While at first it is only dimly aware of its presence in the actual world, or only knows quite simply that this world is its own, it strides forward in this belief to a general appropriation of it own assured possessions, and

plants the symbol of its sovereignty on every height and in every depth. But this superficial "[it is] mine," is not its ultimate interest; the joy of this general appropriation finds still in its possessions the alien "other" which abstract Reason does not contain within itself. Reason is dimly aware of itself as a profounder essence than the pure "I" *is*, and must demand that difference, that being, in its manifold variety, become its very own, that it behold itself as the *actual* world and find itself present as an [outer] shape and Thing. But even if Reason digs into the very entrails of things and opens every vein in them so that it may gush forth to meet itself it will not attain this joy; it must have completed itself inwardly before it can experience the consummation of itself. (146)

Zuerst sich in der Wirklichkeit nur ahnend oder sie nur als das *Ihrige* überhaupt wissend, schreitet sie in diesem Sinne zur allgemeinen Besitznehmung des ihr versicherten Eigentums und pflanzt auf alle Höhen und in alle Tiefen das Zeichen ihrer Souveränität. Aber dieses oberflächliche Mein ist nicht ihr letztes Interesse; die Freude dieser allgemeinen Besitznehmung findet an ihrem Eigentume noch das fremde Andere, das die abstrakte Vernunft nicht an ihr selbst hat. Die Vernunft ahnt sich als ein tieferes Wesen, denn das reine Ich ist und muß fordern, daß der Unterschied, das *mannigfaltige Sein*, ihm als das Seinige selbst werde, daß es sich als die *Wirklichkeit* anschaue und sich als Gestalt und Ding gegenwärtig finde. Aber wenn die Vernunft alle Eingeweide der Dinge durchwühlt und ihnen alle Adern öffnet, daß sie sich daraus entgegenspringen möge, so wird sie nicht zu diesem Glücke gelangen, sondern muß an ihr selbst vorher sich vollendet haben, um dann ihre Vollendung erfahren zu können. (186)

The scientist's observation of nature—a collector's delight, Rousseau's passion for botany and for the classification of natural species, all those great typologies Foucault attributed to the sciences of the "classical age"—these passions harbor a secret frustration, a hidden desperation, as observing Reason, thrusting its hands into the very insides of Nature and churning about within them (*aufwühlen*), is unable in this superficial activity to find itself.

Yet we have not yet touched on what completes and seals, finalizes and confirms that dimension of work or action which can alone certify them as being somehow universal; it is a tricky question, which the example of the universality of language will not particularly help us solve in any simple way. Still, the notion of a work as a message or a communication of some kind inflects our thinking about the production of objects or the performing of an act in an unexpected direction, in which objects presumably ask for some kind of consumption while acts themselves, particularly when they are "world-historical," achieve a very special kind of recognition from other people.

This is at any rate the turn that Hegel's thought takes here, in a shift from the recognition of self that becomes available to me when I externalize myself, to the attention and interest of other people: "actualization is . . . a display of what is one's own in the element of universality, whereby it becomes, and should become, the affair of everyone" (309; 251). This emphasis on the universality of what is truly individual is quite the opposite of that stereotype of the individual versus society which has become a knee-jerk reflex in the Western tradition (and which Hegel explicitly calls a deception here [*Betrug*]):

> It is, then, equally a deception of oneself and of others if it is pretended that what one is concerned with is the "*matter in hand*" *alone*. A consciousness that opens up a subject-matter soon learns that others hurry along like flies to freshly poured-out milk, and want to busy themselves with it; and they learn about that individual that he, too, is concerned with the subject-matter, not as an *object*, but as his *own* affair. On the other hand, if what is supposed to be essential is merely the doing of it, the employment of powers and capacities, or the expression of this particular individuality, then equally it is learned by all parties that they all regard themselves as affected and *invited to participate*, and instead of a mere "doing," or separate action, peculiar to the individual who opened up the subject-matter, something has been opened up that is for others as well, or is a subject-matter on its own account. In both cases the same thing happens and only has a different significance by contrast with what was assumed and was supposed to be accepted. Consciousness experiences both sides as equally essential moments, and in doing so learns what

the *nature* of the "*matter in hand*" really is, viz. that it is neither merely something which stands opposed to action in general, and to individual action, nor action which stands opposed to a continuing being and which would be the free *genus* of these moments as its *species*. Rather is its nature such that its *being* is the action of the single individual and of all individuals and whose action is immediately *for others*, or is a "matter in hand" and is such only as the action of *each* and of *everyone*: the essence which is the essence of all being, viz. *spiritual essence*. (251-252)

Es ist also ebenso Betrug seiner selbst und der anderen, wenn es nur um die *reine Sache* zu tun sein soll; ein Bewußtsein, das eine Sache auftut, macht vielmehr die Erfahrung, daß die anderen, wie die Fliegen zu frisch aufgestellter Milch, herbeieilen und sich dabei geschäftig wissen wollen,—und sie an ihm, daß es ihm ebenso nicht um die Sache als Gegenstand, sondern als um die *seinige* zu tun ist. Hingegen, wenn nur das *Tun selbst*, der Gebrauch der Kräfte und Fähigkeiten oder das Aussprechen dieser Individualität das Wesentliche sein soll, so wird ebenso gegenseitig die Erfahrung gemacht, daß alle sich rühren und für eingeladen halten und statt eines *reinen* Tuns oder eines *einzelnen* eigentümlichen Tuns vielmehr etwas, das ebensowohl für *andere* ist, oder eine Sache selbst aufgetan wurde. Es geschieht in beiden Fällen dasselbe und hat nur einen verschiedenen Sinn gegen denjenigen, der dabei angenommen wurde und gelten sollte. Das Bewußtsein erfährt beide Seiten als gleich wesentliche Momente und hierin was die Natur der Sache selbst ist, nämlich weder nur Sache, welche dem Tun überhaupt und dem einzelnen Tun, noch Tun, welches dem Bestehen entgegengesetzt und die von diesen Momenten als ihren *Arten* freie *Gattung* wäre, sondern ein Wesen, dessen Sein das *Tun* des *einzelnen* Individuums und aller Individuen, und dessen Tun unmittelbar *für andere* oder eine Sache ist und nur Sache ist als *Tun Aller* und *Jeder*; das Wesen, welches as Wesen aller Wesen, das geistige Wesen ist. (309–310)

This unexpected revelation of the collective within individuality and its work will now lead us to two distinct yet fundamental lines of Hegel's thought: the first is, of course, Spirit itself, in whose structure other people, and the universal they define, are constitutive: yet now in an historical way rather than a structural one, giving rise to that series of "shapes" as which we glimpse Hegel's so-called philosophy of history.

The other direction in which the ethos of work and externalization takes us can be said to be metaphysical rather than historical, in the sense in which it registers what seem to be philosophical -isms and worldviews, rather than conjunctures and situations. What is at stake here is the Hegelian conception of immanence, a philosophical commitment that may run deeper than the celebration of an ethic of work and externalization (to which it must however be intimately related) and which will, particularly on the political level, be of great significance in the debate by subsequent generations about the revolutionary or reactionary implications of Hegel's work.

But that debate needs to be prefaced by a different kind of qualification, namely that, despite his familiarity with Adam Smith and emergent economic doctrine,[27] Hegel's conception of work and labor—I have specifically characterized it as a handicraft ideology—betrays no anticipation of the originalities of industrial production or the factory system. And even though one influential strand of the Marxist tradition valorizes work-satisfaction and attempts to ideologize a positive and workerist conception of collective labor, it cannot be said that Hegel's analyses of individual work and production here are easily transferred to the new industrial situation. Marx's concept of the four-fold nature of what he calls alienation[28] cannot be extrapolated from Hegel, although with an intensified dose of negativity it is possible to see the dialectic of Sartre's *Critique* as a more radical development of Hegelian ideas of externalization and internalization, applied to history itself.

---

[27] See Georg Lukács, *The Young Hegel*, Cambridge: MIT Press, 1976.
[28] Karl Marx, *Early Writings*, London: Penguin, 1975, 322–334.

Chapter 7

Immanence

The commitment to immanence declares itself most powerfully, to be sure, in Hegel's wholesale attack on ethics, particularly of the Kantian variety. (It is important to distinguish the technical German term for this philosophical subfield—*Moralität* or morality—from the associations of the word *Sittlichkeit*, which conveys the collective values or mores—*Sitten*—of an historical group or period, and which counts for Hegel as *Geist* or spirit, rather than as mere individual ethics.)

We have already touched on moments in which Hegel puts the *Sollen* or ethical imperative through its philosophical paces and demonstrates its contradictions: for example, that between Nature and duty, conceived of by Kant as unmotivated and as non-pleasurable (for even the pleasure that might be taken in fulfilling one's duty makes of the latter an interested act, and therefore not yet a fully ethical, that is to say, disinterested one). Yet "morality" is meant to bring about some ultimate unity or harmony between Nature and the ethical subject.

> But the consummation of this progress has to be projected into a future infinitely remote; for if it actually came about, this would do away with the moral consciousness. For morality is only moral *consciousness* as negative essence, for whose pure duty sensuousness has only a *negative* significance, is only *not* in conformity with duty. But in that harmony, *morality qua consciousness*, i.e. its *actuality*, vanishes, just as

in the moral consciousness, or in the *actuality* of morality, the *harmony* vanishes. The consummation, therefore, cannot be attained, but is to be thought of merely as an *absolute* task, i.e. one which simply remains a task. (446–447/368)

The dilemma has some resemblance to another, more passionate or existential one, namely that of the so-called law of the heart, where the solitary hero (in other words, Jean-Jacques) pits the authenticity of his own private love and passion against the whole outside world: a reality which is,

> on the one hand a law by which the particular individuality is oppressed, a violent ordering of the world which contradicts the law of the heart, and on the other hand, a humanity suffering under that ordering, a humanity that does not follow the law of the heart, but is subjected to an alien necessity. (275/221)

The individual then seeks the liberation of this humanity from its alienation, seeks to establish the law of the heart as a universal law, at which point his own individuality vanishes, and his passion degenerates into what Hegel ventures to call

> an inner perversion of itself . . . a deranged consciousness which finds that its essential being is immediately non-essential, its reality immediately an unreality . . . The heart-throb for the welfare of humanity therefore passes into the ravings of an insane self-conceit, into the fury of consciousness to preserve itself from destruction . . . (280/225–226)

The immediate reference is clearly the agony of Rousseau in *Rousseau juge de Jean-Jacques*, in which philanthropy and paranoia meet in a desperate dialectical unity.

In both instances, then, an individual ethos meets the otherness of collectivity or the world, and founders on the impossible contradiction of the very notion of "law," recapitulating that earlier dialectic of the inner laws of nature, of "force" or essence and its distinction from appearance. "Law" is a desperate attempt of *Verstand* to think immanence by separating its moments: inside from outside, before from after, cause from effect, possibility from actuality. Indeed, the word actuality—an English translation more pointed and useful than its German equivalent *Wirklichkeit* or reality as such—is a whole Hegelian program here; and we can best approach the Hegelian doctrine of immanence by understanding that for Hegel actuality already includes its own possibilities and potentialities; they are not something separate and distinct from it, lying in some other alternate world or in the future. Qua possibility this promise of the real is already here and not simply "possible."

This dialectic, worked out elaborately in the *Logic*, lies at the very heart of Hegel's realism, in politics and in history alike. It is also the other face of the Hegelian doctrine of necessity, about which he says that philosophy is its study, but of which he also sometimes seems to offer a retrospective view—the owl of Minerva famously taking its flight at dusk—yet insisting that philosophy only has to do "with what is."[29] Yet all of these observations would seem to exclude the future, and in one way or another to stage reality as a temporal present in which there can be no conception of radical change.

This would indeed be a paradoxical outcome for dialectical philosophy; but Hegel's essential conservatism, his alleged defense of the Prussian status quo, has often been plausibly argued, and even if it can be disproven, the refutation would also have to be accompanied by some persuasive demonstration of the ways in which Hegelian immanence can be said to energize a revolutionary frame of mind rather than discourage it and strengthen a kind of disempowered apathy, what he himself might have called "listlessness": "the listless movement of Spirit which no longer creates a distinction within itself" (424/349). Yet what else can be expected from the famous slogan, "what is real is rational and what is rational is real" (certainly a far better characterization of the spirit of Hegelianism than the old tripartite formula)? An apocryphal story has the student Heinrich

---

[29] G. W. F. Hegel, *The Philosophy of History*, trans. J. Sibree, New York: Dover, 1956, 87; and *Elements of the Philosophy of Right*, ed. Allen W. Wood, trans. H. B. Nisbet, Cambridge: Cambridge University Press, 1991, 23.

Heine approaching the Master at the end of a lecture and impertinently asking him whether this formula was not a rather conservative one. Hegel is supposed to have looked down his nose at the upstart and to have observed, "as you are obviously a clever young man, to you alone I will reveal the secret meaning, namely, that the real must become rational, and the rational must become real."

Indeed, it is in this sense that the Left has always understood Hegel's doctrine, thus reinforcing the political ambiguity of his work in general and raising once again the issue of temporality and that of the compatibility of historical change with Hegel's doctrine of immanence. If the real must become rational, then we are apparently back in the world of Kant's ethical imperatives, and all of Hegel's severest strictures fall back on his own positions. In fact, in this reading of Hegel—one affirmed by Marx himself in his own doctrine—the future is already present within the present of time: the present is already immanently the future it "ought" to have. Historical change exists, but it is systemic change; it is the movement between the great Hegelian "shapes" or *Gestalten*, which foreshadow later structural conceptions of the social totality, of epistemes or even modes of production.

This is not to say that such a notion of totality does not remain ambiguous: for the affirmation of the future already latent in the present can mean on the one hand that the future is already here, but waiting within the present as the statue waits to be disengaged from the sculptor's block of marble; or it can simply mean that whatever future is already present in the unsubstantial subjective form of wishes and longings, never to be realized insofar as "the future never comes."

No one can rescue Hegelianism from profound structural ambiguities of this kind, which are clearly indissociable from the unity of opposites. But an emphasis on the ethos of work and activity will at least tend to weigh it in the direction of praxis, as a striking moment in Hegel's early discussion of the religious world (in the section on the Unhappy Consciousness) makes dramatically clear. Hegel is discussing the internal divisions of medieval real life, where "consciousness merely finds itself desiring and working; it is not aware that to find itself active in this way implies that it is in fact certain of itself, and that its feeling of the alien existence is this self-feeling" (170; 132). There follows an extraordinary outburst, in which Hegel affirms that the reality of praxis outweighs any religious ignorance or repression of it:

> The fact that the unchangeable consciousness *renounces* and *surrenders* its embodied form, while, on the other hand, the particular individual consciousness *gives thanks* [for the gift], i.e. *denies* itself the satisfaction of being conscious of its *independence*, and assigns the essence of its action not to itself but to the beyond, through these two moments of *reciprocal self-surrender* of both parts, consciousness does, of course, gain a sense of its *unity* with the Unchangeable. But this unity is at the same time affected with division, is again broken within itself, and from it there emerges once more the antithesis of the universal and the individual. For though consciousness renounces the *show* of satisfying its feeling of self, it obtains the *actual* satisfaction of it; for it *has been* desire, work, and enjoyment; as consciousness it has *willed, acted,* an *enjoyed.* Similarly, even its *giving of thanks*, in which it acknowledges the other extreme as the essential Being and counts itself nothing, is its *own* act which counterbalances the action of the other extreme, and meets the self-sacrificing beneficence with a *like* action. If the other extreme delivers over to consciousness only the *surface* of its being, yet consciousness *also* gives thanks; and in surrendering its own action, i.e. its *essential* being, it really does more than the other which only sheds a superficial element of itself. Thus the entire movement is reflected not only in the actual desiring, working, and enjoyment, but even in the very giving of thanks where the reverse seems to take place, in the *extreme of individuality*. Consciousness feels itself therein as this particular individual, and does not let itself be deceived by its own seeming renunciation, for the truth of the matter is that it has not *renounced* itself. What has been brought about is only the double reflection into the two extremes; and the result is the renewed division into the opposed consciousness of the *Unchangeable*, and the consciousness of willing, performing, and enjoying, and self-renunciation itself which confronts it; in other words, the consciousness of *independent individuality* in general. (134–135)

Daß das unwandelbare Bewußtsein auf seine Gestalt *Verzicht tut* und sie *preisgibt*, dagegen das einzelne Bewußtsein *dankt*, d. h. die Befriedigung des Bewußtseins seiner *Selbständigkeit* sich *versagt* und das Wesen des Tuns von sich ab dem Jenseits zuweist, durch diese beiden Momente des *gegenseitigen Sich-Aufgebens* beider Teile entsteht hiermit allerdings dem Bewußtsein *seine* Einheit mit dem Unwandelbaren. Allein zugleich ist diese Einheit mit der Trennung affiziert, in sich wieder gebrochen, und es tritt aus ihr der Gegensatz des Allgemeinen und Einzelnen wieder hervor. Denn das Bewußtsein entsagt zwar *zum Scheine* der Befriedigung seines Selbstgefühls, erlangt aber die *wirkliche* Befriedigung desselben; denn *es ist* Begierde, Arbeit und Genuß gewesen; *es* hat als Bewußtsein *gewollt*, *getan* und *genossen*. Sein *Danken* ebenso, worin es das andere Extrem als das Wesen anerkennt und sich aufhebt, ist selbst *sein eigenes* Tun, weiches das Tun des andern Extrems aufwiegt und der sich preisgebenden Wohltat ein *gleiches* Tun entgegenstellt; wenn jenes ihm seine *Oberfläche* überläßt, so dankt es *aber auch* und tut darin, indem es sein Tun, d.h. sein *Wesen* selbst aufgibt, eigentlich mehr als das andere, das nur eine Oberfläche von sich abstößt. Die ganze Bewegung reflektiert sich also nicht nur im wirklichen Begehren, Arbeiten und Genießen, sondern sogar selbst im Danken, worin das Gegenteil zu geschehen scheint, in das *Extrem der Einzelheit*. Das Bewußtsein fühlt sich darin als dieses Einzelne und läßt sich durch den Schein seines Verzichtleistens nicht täuschen, denn die Wahrheit desselben ist, daß es sich nicht aufgegeben hat; was zustande gekommen, ist nur die gedoppelte Reflexion in die beiden Extreme, und das Resultat [ist] die wiederholte Spaltung in das entgegengesetzte Bewußtsein des *Unwandelbaren* und in das Bewußtsein des *gegenüberstehenden* Wollens, Vollbringens, Genießens und des auf sich Verzichtleistens selbst oder der *fürsichseienden Einzelheit* überhaupt. (172-173)

Chapter 8

Spirit as Collectivity
(*Antigone*, or the One Into Two)

We must now cross that seemingly decisive boundary that separates the chapters dealing with consciousness and individuality from those explicitly concerned with Spirit or *Geist*, which is to say with collective life as such. In reality, however, this boundary also serves to make clear retroactively how much of the earlier chapters is already implicitly or explicitly interpersonal and even, in some instances, social. For example, it will be necessary to return to the Master/Slave dialectic in order to judge to what degree this "moment" is to be considered an historical event and to what degree it is a persistent structure. Whether these two perspectives can somehow be combined dialectically is an open question—which is to say that it is a question I am tempted to answer negatively.

For qua event the struggle that eventuates in the Master/Slave relationship would seem to be something on the order of a myth, like that notion of a social contract of some kind which seems foreshadowed in it; it is, in other words, a narrative of origins and to that degree would seem, to be, whatever else it is, an illicit form of philosophical thinking, all the more questionable to the degree to which it has genuine rhetorical or representational power. (It should be noted that there seem to be two such myths in Rousseau: alongside his version of contractual origins, we find his denunciation of private property in the *Second Discourse*: "whoever first says, this is *mine* . . .") To be sure, it is possible to consider such a narrative of origins a mere trope (like the opposing one of genealogy), a device for articulating and representing a structure rather than for claiming to stage an event. But at this point it would seem indispensable to consult the richest commentary on this particular episode, namely the historically influential one of Alexandre Kojève, whose lectures (1933–1939) in many ways constituted an explosive reinvention of Hegel leading in too many directions to be exhaustively explored here. Suffice it to say that Kojève's reading can no longer be ours today, in a very different situation from that of the long Cold War of 1917–1989; but that it can be useful in articulating topics and interpretations in which we must distinguish ourselves from him, and in particular that "end of history" which, attributed to him, has most recently been revived.

Indeed, Kojève would seem to have foretold not one, but two ends of history. In one, a convergence between the United States and the Soviet Union concretely realizes Hegel's alleged hypothesis of a "universal and homogeneous state" (145): something which has been interpreted as the inauguration of a classless society. But this is so only if "class" is grasped as a purely social concept and redefined (as Kojève himself does) around the notion of recognition. The more profound historical truth in Kojève's assertion is to be glimpsed only if we understand this decisive moment as the disappearance of the aristocracy and its culture (and the effacement of the peasantry as well). Indeed, we now know that the ancien régime in Europe does not fully disappear until 1944, when the Red Army enters a still semi-feudal Poland and East Prussia (on other post-war world chronologies this moment will generally coincide with agricultural reform).[30] What we call class culture and even class consciousness as such would seem to have been predicated on the self-definition of the bourgeoisie in its opposition to the feudal aristocracies: when these disappear—or where, as in the United States, they never existed in the first place—a rather different socio-cultural form emerges often symptomatized by the tendency to substitute the term "middle classes," a non-economic characterization, for that of the bourgeoisie.

---

[30] See Arno Mayer, *The Persistence of the Old Regime*, New York: Pantheon Books, 1981.

This new universal subject—which today we find everywhere on the post-colonial globe—is democratic not so much in the sense in which each individual is henceforth "recognized" (as Kojève sometimes seems to imply [145–146]) but rather by virtue of that *demand* of each subject for equal recognition and that egalitarian hatred of special status and special privileges that can also be characterized as a plebeian class consciousness and that is to be found in all the populations of the world today and not only in the American "lower middle classes" or the post-Soviet (post-socialist) masses. China too, after the Cultural Revolution, emerged as a population stripped of the old pre-revolutionary reflexes; and the Indian theorization of subalternity also has as its object another such a "homogeneous and universal" individuality (which is clearly not incompatible with the rush to make money in the new world system). But it is important not to confuse this henceforth mass cultural mentality with the economic conception of social class, nor to attribute to it either the end of class struggle or the emergence of some new kind of radical-democratic impulse on the political level. As for the end of revolution and ideology which Kojève is also supposed to have foretold in his theorization of the "end of history," it seems clear enough that in globalization and postmodernity these will not take the same forms they wore historically in a world in which remnants of the ancien régime still persisted (or in other words in the period we still call modernity).

The other end of history theorized by Kojève takes shape in his reading of Absolute Spirit, which he wishes to represent in some anthropomorphic way as he did in his evocation of Napoleon (to which we will return). It is indeed not altogether clear whether the triumph of Napoleon (or later on, Stalin, or still later for Kojève, de Gaulle) figures the narrative climax and completion of the revolutionary process, or whether the supreme allegorical realization of that process is not rather to be found in that ultimate philosophical embodiment which Kojève theorizes as the Sage (and perhaps indeed one can even sense a hesitation in him between the two which at certain points coalesces into the traditional philosopher-king). Kojève is surely right insistently to remind his academic public that the figure of Napoleon is fundamental for the *Phenomenology* and carries within itself, for Hegel, all the rich promise of the French Revolution itself. Nor should we forget that Hegel wrote this book long before the fall of Napoleon and the unexpected triumph of European reaction that confronted him for the rest of his career; just as Kojève himself lectured at the flood-tide of Stalin's power and promise (and long before his own conversion to Gaullism and then to the European Union, let alone the dissolution of the USSR). As for the Sage, however, I feel it is essential for us to deal with the moment of Absolute Spirit in such a way that it is not personified in any particular anthropomorphic figure or "centered subject," let alone reified into a separate historical stage or moment in its own right.

With these qualifications, we may return to Kojève's path-breaking reinterpretation of the *Phenomenology*, but not before we have come to terms more directly with its conception of Spirit as such: "with this [self-consciousness]," Hegel says, almost as though he had in mind the present investigation, "we already have before us the Notion of Spirit. What still lies ahead for consciousness is the experience of what Spirit is—this absolute substance which is the unity of the different independent self-consciousnesses which, in their opposition, enjoy perfect freedom and independence: 'I' that is 'We' that is 'I'" (145/110), a condition elsewhere described as "the reconciliation of its individuality with the universal" (165/128), a starkly oversimplified formula with which it would be best to remain unsatisfied, all the while remembering that we have already identified the universal with language rather than with some reified entity imagined to be the social totality.

Indeed, such "reconciliation" is not at all to be understood in terms of the stereotypical struggle between the individual and "society"; but rather glimpsed at an earlier moment in which society as an entity has not yet really coalesced. This is, indeed, what the famous *Antigone* chapter gives us to witness, as it serves as a first panel—the emergence of the polis now conceived as pre-modern or even tribal society—in a triptych which pointedly excludes the Middle Ages (already referenced in the Unhappy Consciousness), jumping ahead to secular (or emergent "modern") society in the period of absolute monarchy, and then the revolutionary moment of 1789 and the end of the old regime.

I will not comment at any great length on Hegel's reading of Sophocles' play, which has already given rise to an elaborated tradition still very much alive today[31]: I do side with those who following the later Hegel's insistence on the necessarily equivalent positions of Antigone and Creon, and on the implication that tragedy always presupposes an irresolvable historical conflict between two forces that destroy each other. For on Hegel's reading, not only is Creon himself destroyed along with his victim, but with both the very form of the polis is itself irredeemably shattered (necessarily giving way to that very different expansion of a single triumphant city-state into the Roman Empire). The tragedy called *Antigone* is therefore a contemplation of history as such, in all its most irreconcilable singularity: no synthesis can come of this moment, no optimistic theodicy can encompass it, not even the success story of the State as such; *Antigone* testifies to the existence of problems that cannot be solved, and as such utterly invalidates the myth of Hegel as a teleological thinker.

But the most enlightening dialectical feature of Hegel's reading lies not in its culmination but in its point of departure. Alain Badiou has frequently insisted on what one may call the Maoist side of Hegel's political thought: in particular, the philosopher's support of the maxim, "One into Two."[32] The most immediate evidence for this surprising assertion is to be found, indeed, in the political doctrine, where Hegel asserts an even more surprising position, namely that parties are strengthened by internal schisms—an idea that will astonish anyone with some experience in practical politics, where the appeal for unity so often overrides the demand for ideological

---

[31] On the *Antigone*, see also Hegel's later thoughts in the *Aesthetics*, Oxford: Oxford University Press, 1975, 1217-1218; Jacques Lacan, *Le séminaire, livre VII: L'Ethique de la psychanalyse*, Paris: Éditions de Seuil, 1986; as well as Alenka Zupančič, *Ethics of the Real*, London: Verso, 2000; and Judith Butler, *Antigone's Claim*, New York: Columbia University Press, 2000.

[32] See above, note 16.

purity. Hegel seems to mean that an internal split or schism betokens the interiorization of a conflict that would otherwise have remained external and have opposed two radically different kinds of groups. Now, however, it is the same group which is divided on a given issue, so that the latter can be appropriated in a different and more satisfactory way. He does not seem to foresee that process of infinite fission into smaller and smaller groups or sects, which has been so notable in left politics in the US and elsewhere; it should on the other hand be remembered that this process of internal division is to be dialectically related to the purely formal unity of the monarchy itself (and also that political parties—hitherto classically denounced as "factions"— were then still in an early stage of their development in the West). This first practical political celebration of "One into Two" can thus be seen as an attempt to replace a transcendental difference with an immanent one.

The instantiation of the principle that concerns us here is rather a social one, and, if you like, an early example of what Luhmann would have called differentiation. Indeed, what I want to argue is that the primordial opposition the *Phenomenology's Antigone* chapter seems to stage should rather be understood as the emergence of an articulated society as such. It would seem that for Hegel we must imagine those first human collectivities that precede the emergence of organized societies as mere "simple substance": they have as yet no articulated content, since content can only be generated by differentiation itself. Such social groups are something like the collective equivalent of that abstract reason or abstract unity we have already confronted in figures like epistemological consciousness or that empire in which there exists only one individual (the despot).

But Hegel's watchword—we have already quoted it before—is that of a negativity which is in this respect fundamentally division (his scorn being reserved for that "difference which is no difference," and which therefore "makes no difference"): "Spirit is, in its simple truth, consciousness, and forces its moments apart"—"schlägt seine Momente auseinander" (327/266). He reads this first moment of the community in terms of an opposition between consciousness and self-consciousness; but as we have seen, this is only one possible thematization of the pure form of opposition and in our present chapter it will quickly be replaced by a different one.

Spirit is, in its simple truth, consciousness, and forces its moments apart. *Action* divides it into substance, and consciousness of the substance; and divides the substance as well as consciousness. Substance, as the universal essence and End, stands over against the *individualized* reality; the infinite middle term is self-consciousness which, being the implicit unity of itself and substance, now becomes that unity explicitly and unites the universal essence and its individualized reality. The latter it raises to the former and acts *ethically*, the former it brings down to the latter and realizes the End, the substance which had an existence only in thought. It brings into existence the unity of its self and substance as its own work, and thus as an actual existence.

In this separation of the moments of consciousness, the simple substance has, on the one hand, preserved the antithesis to self-consciousness, and on the other, it equally exhibits in its own self the nature of consciousness, viz. to create distinctions within itself, exhibiting itself as a world articulated into its [separate] spheres. It thus splits itself up into distinct ethical substances, into a human and a divine law. Similarly, the self-consciousness confronting the substance assigns to itself according to its nature one of these powers, and as a knowing, is on the one hand ignorant of what it does, and on the other knows what it does, a knowledge which for that reason is a deceptive knowledge. It learns through its own act the contradiction of those powers into which the substance divided itself and their mutual downfall, as well as the contradiction between *its* knowledge of the ethical character of its action, and what is in its own proper nature ethical, and thus finds its own downfall. In point of fact, however, the ethical substance has developed through this process into actual self-consciousness; in other words, this particular self has become the actuality of what it is in essence; but precisely in this development the ethical order has been destroyed. (266)

Der Geist ist in seiner einfachen Wahrheit Bewußtsein und schlägt seine Momente auseinander. Die *Handlung* trennt ihn in die Substanz und das Bewußtsein derselben und trennt ebensowohl die Substanz als das Bewußtsein. Die Substanz tritt, als allgemeines *Wesen* und *Zweck*, sich als der *vereinzelten* Wirklichkeit gegenüber; die unendliche Mitte ist das Selbstbewußtsein, welches, *an sich* Einheit seiner und der Substanz, es nun *für sich* wird, das allgemeine Wesen und seine vereinzelte Wirklichkeit vereint, diese zu jenem erhebt und sittlich handelt—und jenes zu dieser herunterbringt und den Zweck, die nur gedachte Substanz ausführt; es bringt die Einheit seines Selbsts und der Substanz als *sein Werk* und damit als *Wirklichkeit* hervor.

In dem Auseinandertreten des Bewußtseins hat die einfache Substanz den Gegensatz teils gegen das Selbstbewußtsein erhalten, teils stellt sie damit ebensosehr an ihr selbst die Natur des Bewußtseins, sich in sich selbst zu unterscheiden, als eine in ihre Massen gegliederte Welt dar. Sie spaltet sich also in ein unterschiedenes sittliches Wesen, in ein menschliches und göttliches Gesetz. Ebenso das ihr gegenübertretende Selbstbewußtsein teilt sich nach seinem Wesen der einen dieser Mächte zu, und als Wissen in die Unwissenheit dessen, was es tut, und in das Wissen desselben, das deswegen ein betrogenes Wissen ist. Es erfährt also in seiner Tat sowohl den Widerspruch jener *Mächte*, worein die Substanz sich entzweite, und ihre gegenseitige Zerstörung, wie den Widerspruch seines Wissens von der Sittlichkeit seines Handelns mit dem, was an und für sich sittlich ist, und findet *seinen eigenen* Untergang. In der Tat aber ist die sittliche Substanz durch diese Bewegung zum *wirklichen Selbstbewußtsein* geworden oder *dieses* Selbst zum *An und Fürsich* seienden; aber darin ist eben die Sittlichkeit zugrunde gegangen. (327–8)

We must therefore initially read the opposition between "human law and divine law" not as a struggle between the state and the family or clan that tears society apart; but first and foremost as the division which brings society itself into being in the first place by articulating its first great differentiations, that of warrior versus priest, or of city versus clan, or even outside versus inside. Here the empirical laws of daily life find themselves doubled by a "beyond" of sacred law and commandment: the sacred finds as it were its empirical place in the family blood line, while secular power comes into its own in the palace. Each of these larval powers brings the other into being and reinforces the distinctiveness of its opposite number: a human law is not possible without a divine law and vice versa. This will be a paradox only for those for whom a disintegrating society is somehow the opposite of a successful and enduring one: for Hegel's point here is precisely that of the mortality of social forms. What is affirmed is that the contradiction which ultimately tears the polis apart and destroys it, leaving it vulnerable, first to Macedonian and then to Roman power, is the same opposition that brings it into being as a viable structure in the first place. The unique form of the city-state is also what ultimately dooms it; and we will make the point later on, not only that this has to do with size, but that the dialectic is itself to be grasped in terms of perpetual expansion.

For the moment, however, it will be readily grasped that Hegel's fascination with the *Antigone*—whatever his comments on the character herself—has to do with the cunning with which Sophocles has been able to situate both dimensions of the opposition within the unity of a single family: the embodiment of the state and the embodiment of the laws of the underworld are uncle and niece (it is a difference within an identity that will later on fascinate readers and spectators of the same author's *Oedipus tyrannus*; and it would also be tempting to speculate on the dramatic potentialities of uncles in general—as in *Hamlet* or in the anthropology of matriarchy). At the same time, the qualitative differences within this representation—as testified by the tendency to admire Antigone and to find Creon a relatively weak and inept embodiment of state power—are themselves the expression of the incommensurability of the two dimensions at odds here: Creon's combination of rigidity and vacillation is clearly very different from the heroic determination and melancholy of Antigone, as different as beauty is, not necessarily from ugliness, but from awkwardness and gracelessness, from the externality of caricature and of state rhetoric. It is as if two radically distinct modes of representation were marshaled within a single representational project, betraying their more fundamental structural variance by way of the appearance of mere stylistic distinction.

But here too the dialectic of identity and difference cuts across all these levels: it is the original unity of the two levels into which the social substance has divided that allows them to be represented within a unified narrative; while it is the radical distance from each other of the irreconcilable forces in question that strains at the representational surface and generates that dissonance that expresses the unified meaning of tragic contradiction. The fragility of the polis lies precisely in its capacity to incorporate and to internalize these two uniquely different powers and dimensions that will eventually tear it apart, as opposed to older sacred societies or more modern secular states which do not include the same fatal tensions.

At the same time, it is important to remember that the dissolution of the polis also means the disappearance of that specific thematization or content in which its contradiction was expressed: thus, although there will later on be structural analogies between the opposition of human and divine law staged in the *Antigone*, such as the pre-revolutionary (eighteenth century) conflict between Enlightenment and Belief, such parallels should—following the idea of variations without a theme—never be reified into some more general or global thesis about religion, but rather historicized to the point at which each opposition becomes a unique singularity. That it is exceedingly difficult to keep faith with this methodological advice not only poses difficulties for the reader/interpreter but conveys the far greater magnitude of Hegel's own form-problem: he must somehow give content to his own analyses without perpetuating that content, allowing it to multiply into the thematics of any number of oppositions without allowing the terms of any of those oppositions to harden over into a specific philosophical thesis. Meanwhile, he must also practice the dialectical exercise of such oppositions without allowing the method to become reified either, as it does in structuralist doctrine, and as it threatens to do even in the characterization of it as dialectical (a word he avoids as much as possible, as we have seen).

Differences without positive terms, as has been observed: but one may also characterize the method as the deconstructive evasion of positive propositions, or that Frankfurt School suspicion of positivisms and of affirmative positions of all kinds (for them "ideological," for the philosophers of Hegel's period "dogmatic"). A somewhat different defamiliarization of all this is offered by Michael Forster's *Hegel and Skepticism*, which usefully demonstrates the kinship between the Hegelian critique of *Verstand* (or externalized and reified thinking) and the *equipollence* of ancient skepticism, which set itself the task of inventing the most persuasive arguments against any affirmative position or proposition.

As against these methodological analogies, we must also set Hegel's own dictum, that subjectivity must always divide; or in other words that it must always become concrete by dividing itself, which is to say that it must always give itself the thematic content of a specific opposition. We cannot, in other words, fulfill such injunctions against positivity by persisting in indeterminacy: we must give ourselves over to the determinate and make our way through such specific content and thematics until we come out the other side—a requirement that seems to me to distinguish this dialectic from the more absolute skepticism of deconstruction. Indeed, we find that if we persevere long enough in the terms of a given moment's opposition, those terms undo themselves, to be sure giving rise to new ones. But this process of flux and perpetual transformation and fission must not itself be reified into a philosophical or sociological notion, as Luhmann does with his named concept of differentiation (whose kinship with the traditional dialectic he freely acknowledges).[33]

Meanwhile, the more difficult problem lies, not in the dissolution of a given opposition and its historical transformation into something else, so much as in the beginning of the whole process: are we to imagine, in other words, and as our own exposition here has tended to suggest, that before the *Antigone* contradiction, the social or Spirit was a kind of amorphous unity, "without shape or form"? That would be a mythical narrative, insofar as there has always been a social order of some kind (or rather, insofar as there has never been an origin of collectivity any more than there has been an origin of language). It is a conundrum which only the concept of "positing" can effectively address: for just as we always posit the anteriority of a nameless object along with the name or idea we have just articulated, so also in the matter of historical temporality we always posit the preexistence of a formless object which is the raw material of our

---

[33] Niklas Luhmann, *The Differentiation of Society*, New York: Columbia University Press, 1982, 305.

emergent social or historical articulation. Hegel tends in such textual moments to have recourse to what were evidently scientific terms in his period. Thus at one point in the "observation of nature" he speaks of "predicates . . . found only as universals, as in truth they are; because of this self-subsistence they get the name of 'matters' [*Materien*], which are neither bodies nor properties . . ." (195/153). At another point, in a more socio-historical context, he uses the term *Massen* (masses):

> The distinctions in essence itself are not accidental determinatenesses; on the contrary, in virtue of the unity of essence and self-consciousness (this being the only possible source of disparity), they are "masses" articulated into groups by the life of the unity which permeates them . . . (321/261)

Finally, at the even more crucial moment in which secularization (or modernity) comes into being, we are treated to an elaborate allegorical digression on the elements ("in the same way Nature displays itself in the universal elements of Air, Water, Fire and Earth" [366; 300]).

I think that these relatively inchoate figures are designed to designate themselves as inchoate (they are thus as terms self-referential allegories whose imprecision as words is also meant to convey the imprecision of what they thus presuppose). They suggest something of what might today be understood as social "levels," a word that, unlike Hegel's, has the disadvantage of being too precise and threatens to turn into a concept or social theory of some kind. For all such words obey a kind of retroactive paradox in which it is the articulation that produces the afterimage of the object it ends up naming (but which did not, of course, exist in that form before the name). "The self knows itself as actual," as Hegel puts it, "only as a transcended self" (365/299), where the term *aufgehoben* designates just this constructivist quasi-temporal paradox of the positing of an object by way of what conceptually brings it into being in the first place.

If you like, the opposition matter-form can be usefully deployed here, provided it is kept under brackets. For this narrative-temporal paradox (or singularity) is not only a solution to the problems posed by critical resistance to mythic narratives of origin (like Hölderlin's notion of the primal *Ur-teilung* which so many historians of philosophy today have taken as itself the mythic origin of German objective idealism[34]); it is also one in which the emergence of a specific historical form retroactively calls into existence the hitherto formless matter from which it has been fashioned. This is a paradox which has no doubt only become conceptualized as such in contemporary philosophy, but which it is on this particular reading plausible to attribute to Hegel himself as a substitute for that "teleology" for which he is ordinarily indicted.

Hegel's compositional struggle will then consist fully as much in a resistance to the reifying power of binary oppositions as it will in their deployment. Here, what has already been said bears repeating, namely that it is in the multiplication of such oppositions that this strategy of dereification is most successful: thus Hegel's next chapter, the rich extended analysis of secularity ("self-alienated Spirit") begins with an opposition between the nobility (also understood in a Nietzschean way as the production of the "noble" or the "good") and the emergent monarchy. But this dialectic of multiplicity and unity, which also rehearses that between center and margin, swiftly evolves into something rather different, which is a nascent contradiction between state power and wealth. Meanwhile, these varying oppositions, which as they play on each other back and forth also become the opposition between the various oppositions, are complicated by the transversal intersection of a wholly new entity, namely language itself as a kind of third term or unstable mediation within and between all of them: thus, the relation of the feudal barons to that primus inter pares who is the king will be that of the language of counsel. The relationship of courtiers to the absolute monarch (Louis XIV) will then become that of the language of flattery; while the supersession of the state by sheer wealth in the eighteenth century opens the door to the delirious language of *Rameau's Nephew*, in which flattery unexpectedly swells into mimicry, artistic genius and Sadean crime.

---

[34] See above, note 9.

We may take the final avatar of this peculiarly protean phenomenon which for convenience we name language to be the incorporation of the absolute negativity of revolutionary Enlightenment into language or culture (*Bildung*) as such, and its devastation of actuality in a way comparable to the devastation by ancient skepticism of ideality. If the historical references of this chapter draw its moments in the direction of contingency and universalizable singularity, the rhythm of oppositions that informs its various contradictions invites us to a pattern of philosophical abstraction, and to a formalization of dialectic that we cannot satisfactorily complete. Indeed, what is essential here is the perpetuation of this tension between the historical and the abstract-philosophical, rather than its resolution one way or the other. We must equally resist the transformation of such complexities into sheer historical facts—history, Hegel tells us, always demonstrating the necessity of contingency itself—as well as their reduction to purely formalistic concepts such as Luhmannian "differentiation."

Once again, the term "thematization" offers a useful way of registering the moment when such constitutive tensions are tendentially reified in either direction. But that the injunction to keep faith with tension and contradiction is not some facile and comfortable postmodern relaxation on "*l'oreiller du doute*" may be judged by the problem Marxist readers will have in placing class struggle within this Hegelian framework: for class struggle as such certainly strikes us as a thematization par excellence, as a triumph of (Marxist) philosophy or system over postmodern theory, if not indeed the shadow of a veritable metaphysics of the social. Marxists will be understandably reluctant to abandon the notion of the primacy of class struggle for formalist positions like that of Laclau and Mouffe for which class or economics can be sometimes be a determinant of political struggle but also sometimes not, and for which therefore the "ultimately determining instance" of these Marxian themes is philosophically and politically unacceptable. All the more does this problem become relevant in the Hegelian framework when we confront the thesis, unavoidable since Kojève's path-breaking readings, that the Master/Slave opposition is Hegel's inscription of class struggle and thereby his explicit anticipation of the Marxian problematic.

The textual problem posed by such a reading of the Master/Slave contradiction offers a choice between grasping the latter as a specific historical situation in an identifiable chronology (thus for example the emergence of an opposition of rich and poor in the ancient city-state) and the hypothesis of Kojève (for which there is no textual evidence) that the opposition of Master and Slave persists throughout the rest of history and subtends Hegel's more explicit historical references much as a musical ground bass might continue on through all kinds of new thematic events in the score. This contention can be rescued, I think, by pointing to a fundamental duality or ambivalence in the idea of recognition itself.

For it can certainly be argued that the Master/Slave structure persists on into the development around *Rameau's Nephew*, where the relationship between rich patron and genial parasite enriches it with new accents and new possibilities. The parasite—Rameau himself—is certainly obliged to work hard in his wit and inventiveness to satisfy the patron; yet the secret dependence of the patron on his retinue is also explicitly brought out, and in particular the former's mortal ennui without his jester, his requirement of distraction as well as of services of all kinds, alongside the all-important never-ending flattery with which this unique kind of slave tirelessly provides his master. Still, we have not worked through the *Bildung* or Culture section of the *Phenomenology* in vain, and we now understand that, given the foregrounding of language as a fundamental social mediation, we must distinguish between such cultural "work" and the labor on matter the older kind of slave provided (and still provides).

That this ambivalence anticipates the traditional Marxian distinction between base and superstructure is evident: its presence within the concept of recognition is most persuasively argued by Forster, who shows that the Master/Slave moment in the *Phenomenology* is to be grasped within the larger context of Hegel's successive explanations for the historical disintegration of the polis (or, what is the same thing, for the emergence of modernity): thus the explanation by way of the Master/Slave opposition is accompanied in earlier works on Christianity by the class division of rich and poor (and in later ones by the distinction between consciousness and self-consciousness).[35] Yet it is already clear in its fundamental elaboration in the *Phenomenology* that the struggle for recognition will be followed by labor and production as such and by the structural distinction of owners and workers: if it is understood that in a dialectical sense the struggle for recognition has never been completed, then recognition and class struggle will indeed end up coinciding.

The problem can then be approached from another direction, namely that of the critique of a politics of recognition and of an insistence on the radical difference between a class politics and the kinds of identity politics the concept of recognition seems to imply or accompany. This is not to say that recognition is always a matter of liberal tolerance: indeed, I would want to argue that the culmination in contemporary thought of this Hegelian theme is to be found in Frantz Fanon's notion of "redemptive violence" which, developing out of the Sartrean notion of otherness as conflict, posits a second moment of the Master/Slave struggle in which the Slave rises against the Master and compels recognition in the form of fear very much in the spirit and the letter of Hegel's initial text. But Fanon is speaking from the situation of colonization, and the actors here—colonial subjects, imperial masters—are easily assimilable to class protagonists. In the case of contemporary or postmodern identity politics, recognition secures the access of the hitherto victimized or oppressed group to the acknowledged status of a new player within an ongoing social system and for the most part to corporate existence (if not codified secession) rather than to assimilation.

To what degree, then, can class struggle itself in its more classic form be grasped as a Hegelian struggle for recognition? One plausible and relatively empirical way of dealing with this dilemma is to insert it within the very idea of class itself and to respect the distinction theoretically alert historians have observed (using a kind

---

[35] See Michael N. Forster, *Hegel and Skepticism*, Cambridge: Harvard University Press, 1989, 53.

of demotic "Hegelian" formula) between a class-in-itself and a class-for-itself. It is a distinction which then reorients the problem around the emergence of class consciousness (the "making" of a class as a self-conscious political agent, in E. P. Thompson's formula) rather than on the structural fact of class division and function on the one hand, or the cultural and superstructural phenomenology of achieved class consciousness on the other. For this second distinction is very much that of the traditional Marxian opposition of base and superstructure, the emphasis on emergence serving as a perhaps equally traditional mediation between the two traditional versions.

Yet from that older perspective, Hegelian recognition would seem to fall on the cultural or superstructural, phenomenological side of the divide, and to risk effacing the more concrete conditions of economic exploitation and of the structure of production as such. Indeed, it may well be asked to what degree class consciousness is a matter of recognition in the first place: it is not at all clear that the dynamic of working-class consciousness turns on its recognition of the bosses as such. One could make a stronger case for its opposite number, ruling-class consciousness, which generally comes into being as a political project when the threats of the emergence of a working class are first registered, in such a way that the consciousness of the latter—in Hegelian terms, the recognition of the Slave as an existence and a danger—precedes the consciousness of the Master as an organized ideology. But this is perhaps to underestimate the existence of that other form of oppositional class consciousness which precedes the emergence of industrial labor and expresses itself in the rage against hierarchy and the arrogance of status and against the haughtiness and ostentation of the elites and the enforcement of caste-like distinctions and prohibitions. This kind of passionate lived class indignation seems from one standpoint to be far more "cultural" than a modern working-class consciousness, and also explicitly to include the struggle with the other within itself by positing the reciprocity of the class enemy—the constitutive insolence of the aristocracy—within its own structure. For the elites themselves, perhaps, the equivalent of such consciousness might be identified as snobbery, a milder but no less interpersonal class feeling. My own sense is that these fundamental class passions, driven by hatred and resentment and seething through all earlier literature, only become "cultural" or superstructural in the narrower sense after caste is replaced by class in the era of industrial capitalism. They certainly persist, however, and one can still observe their lineaments in the radical-democratic passion for social equality as well as in the mediatic temptation of the wish-fulfillments of privilege, in which the older opposition between rich and poor has not yet been superceded by the class identification in terms of exploitation—in other words, in which the sense of social hierarchy has not been superceded by the awareness of economic structure.

The basic ambivalence of the dyad class-in-itself/class-for-itself can meanwhile also explain why the Master/Slave structure (if it persists throughout Hegel's various "moments" or historical shapes, as Kojève argues) is not always visible as such. To return to a musical analogy, this structure would be like an accord that sinks into the harmonic ground at various moments, overlaid with seemingly unrelated developments in the melodic line, yet ever on the point of return and reaffirmation. The persistence will be clearer if we translate this moment into an abstract version of its categorical structure, without losing sight of its concrete social content. The Master/Slave dialectic is then to be grasped as a play of essential and inessential, which is however already a unity of opposites, so that the Master, self-evidently the essential term, is always secretly menaced by his own deeper inessentiality and by the essential work, fear and production of the Slave. This dialectical ambivalence then clearly returns in the *Antigone*, in which a seemingly essential state power is in reality displaced and overturned by Antigone's essential sacrifice. But here already other features or levels of the foundational moment have begun to shift: for although Antigone herself remains the place of self-consciousness, her identification is with the family and the private realm of the household, and no longer with work or production as such.

It is a shift then perpetuated in the most dizzying fashion in the long history of secularization, in which the barons are first essential and then inessential and displaced by the new royal center, itself slowly crowded out by the centrality of money. The position of the slave has now become sheer sycophancy, the former feudal barons becoming mere parasites and court jesters at Versailles, their function then officially assumed in the eighteenth century by the retinue of professional flatterers dramatized by *Rameau's Nephew*. The slave's production, only briefly celebrated at its handicraft apogee in the discussion of the *Sache selbst*, has seemingly become the invisible ground of social life itself: a daily labor taken for granted and henceforth unthematized by bourgeois philosophy, save in one form to which we will return later. How to find it, for example, in the penultimate struggle between Enlightenment and faith?

If we consider that both are "spiritual" entities, that is to say, figures of consciousness rather than of power or domination, we may well find ourselves admitting that either could occupy the structural place of the Slave: faith because Christianity was essentially a slave religion in the first place, and certainly occupied a position of inessentiality with respect to the Unchangeable (in the Unhappy Consciousness); the Enlightenment ("pure insight") insofar as its *Encyclopedia* attempted to incorporate the whole range of practical knowledges and handicrafts and to offer a kind of working guide to the arts and sciences of the day (and even the place of the philosopher—Diderot's "I"—has been compromised by its dialectical relationship with the parasite Rameau, who outdoes his interlocutor in sheer intellectual energy, self-consciousness and know-how).

But to stress this second option is to turn the French Revolution into something like a slave uprising against the clerical power and its royal ally, and to miss one of Hegel's most tantalizing subplots or variants, one which will again take us back to the theme of language. Language has, to be sure, been present throughout these historical developments, in the flattery of the aristocrats as well as that of Rameau himself. Now, however, in Enlightenment, a curious turn is taken in which language is characterized as an infection, as a kind of virus or disease germ. At first, the strange comparison seems to be merely a way of emphasizing the vulnerability of orality (you cannot shut your ears the way you shut your eyes) and the irresistible inter-personality of the medium itself: "The 'I' that utters itself is heard or perceived; it is an infection [*Ansteckung*] in which it has immedi-ately passed into unity with those for whom it is a real existence . . ." (376/309). So far so good: but the alarming terminology will not be alleviated by the reminder of language's affiliation with the protean negativity of consciousness itself which (as in skepticism) takes "the form of a restless process which attacks and pervades the passive essence of the 'matter at hand' [eliminating] everything objective that supposedly stands over against consciousness" (393/323). It is as a calm and persevering unity that faith attempts to stem this rest-less and universal negativity, and it is into this struggle that language then once again decisively intervenes as the common element which explains why "the communication between them is direct and their giving and receiving is an unimpeded flow of each into the other" (420/331). Language has now become something like Habermas's "public sphere" (*Öffentlichkeit*), and

> it is on this account that the communication of "pure insight" is compa-rable to a silent expansion, or to the diffusion, say, of a perfume in the unresisting atmosphere. It is a penetrating infection which does not make itself noticeable beforehand as something opposed to the indif-ferent element into which it insinuates itself, and therefore cannot be warded off. Only when the infection has become widespread is that consciousness [faith], which unheedingly yielded to its influence, aware of it. (402–403; 331)

Or we may think of the expansion of the public sphere, in which "ideas in the air" become insensibly transmitted to the wider publics and the lower classes. At any rate, the triumph of Enlightenment and its revolution is secured by the incapacity of a "one" without content to resist the "many" of social and productive multiplicity.

Yet at this point, with the defeat of "faith," the difference between belief and its opposite number vanishes; and with this "difference without a difference" we enter into the universal domination of absolute freedom, or in other words, revolution as such. But at this point we have also begun to approach Hegel's own present: like that horizon over which the ancient mariners feared to reach the end of the world itself. It is that horizon we must now interrogate as Kojève famously evokes it in his idea of "the end of history."

Chapter 9

Revolution and the "End of History"

It is here, indeed, that the old Master/Slave dialectic reappears for one last time, before Kojève's "universal and homogeneous state" would seem to have put an end to both masters and slaves and to issue in the era of plebeian equality: an astute prediction of universal convergence which for modern readers only—but significantly—omits the leveling function of mass culture. For more traditional readers, however, Hegel's historical narrative will appear to have reached its climax in the rather Kantian evocation of morality, or in other words, in the emergence of a kind of inner-directed citizenship. In order to correct this impression, it will be necessary to take a step backwards in historical time.

The pages on the French Revolution are among the most celebrated in the *Phenomenology*: they theorize the absolute negativity of Rousseau's General Will, in which no middle term is available between the absolute subject and the individual self, so that their only relationship can be that of "unmediated negation": "the sole work and deed of universal freedom is therefore death . . . the coldest and meanest of deaths, with no more significance than cutting off a head of cabbage or swallowing a mouthful of water" (436/360). For in the unison of the revolutionary One, we have lost the productiveness of that division—the one becoming two, the differentiation and articulation of the social substance into its various opposites—that inaugurated the reign of the social, or the collective, or "spirit," at the beginning of Hegel's narrative.

Yet he is anxious to avoid the implication of a cyclical vision of history:

> Out of this tumult, spirit would be thrown back to its starting-point, to the ethical and real world of culture, which would have been merely refreshed and rejuvenated by the fear of the lord and master which has again entered men's hearts. Spirit would have to traverse anew and continually repeat this cycle of necessity if the result were only the complete interpenetration of self-consciousness and Substance—an interpenetration in which self-consciousness, which has experienced the negative power of its universal essence acting on it, would desire to know and find itself, not as this particular individual, but only as a universal, and therefore, too, would be able to endure the objective reality of universal Spirit, a reality excluding self-consciousness *qua* particular. But in absolute freedom there was no reciprocal action between a consciousness that is immersed in the complexities of existence, or that sets itself specific aims and thoughts, and a valid *external* world, whether of reality or thought; instead, the world was absolutely in the form of consciousness as a universal will, and equally self-consciousness was drawn together out of the whole expanse of existence or manifested aims and judgements, and concentrated into the simple self. The culture to which it attains in interaction with that essence is, therefore, the grandest and the last, is that of seeing its pure, simple reality immediately vanish and pass away into empty nothingness. (361–362)

Der Geist wäre aus diesem Tumulte zu seinem Ausgangs-punkte, der sittlichen und realen Welt der Bildung, zurückgeschleudert, welche durch die Furcht des Herrn, die wieder in die Gemüter gekommen, nur erfrischt und verjüngt worden. Der Geist müßte diesen Kreislauf der Notwendigkeit von neuem durchlaufen und immer wiederholen, wenn nur die vollkommene Durchdringung des Selbstbewußtseins und der Substanz das Resultat wäre—eine Durchdringung, worin das Selbstbewußtsein, das die gegen es negative Kraft seines allgemeinen Wesens erfahren, sich nicht als dieses Besondere, sondern nur als Allgemeines wissen und finden wollte und daher auch die gegenständliche, es als Besondere ausschließende Wirklichkeit des allgemeinen Geistes ertragen könnte.—Aber in der absoluten Freiheit war weder das Bewußtsein, das in mannigfaltiges Dasein versenkt ist oder das sich bestimmte Zwecke und Gedanken festsetzt, noch eine *äußere* geltende Welt, es sei der Wirklichkeit oder des Denkens, miteinander in Wechselwirkung, sondern die Welt schlechthin in der Form des Bewußtseins, als allgemeiner Wille, und ebenso das Selbstbewußtsein zusammengezogen aus allem ausgedehnten Dasein oder mannigfaltigem Zweck und Urteil in das einfache Selbst. Die Bildung, die es in der Wechselwirkung mit jenem Wesen erlangt, ist daher die erhabenste und letzte, seine reine einfache Wirklichkeit unmittelbar verschwinden und in das leere Nichts übergehen zu sehen. (438–9)

Hegel seems to want to conclude this historical process with a humanization of the external world: the post-revolutionary subject now has an awareness of self-conscious spirit it did not have when the experience of history was some mere external and incomprehensible necessity and constraint. Now Spirit knows itself to be a universal will: "the universal will is its pure knowing and willing [*reines Wissen und Wollen*] and it is the universal will qua this knowing and willing" (440/363); and with this collective self-consciousness Hegel is content to pass to its purely individual form as morality (or citizenship): we may assume he thought its collective action would take the form of the framing of constitutions.

But as we have seen, Hegel is only approaching that absolute historical present which is the end of his world: 1807 is only the dawning of the Napoleonic consolidation of the Revolution which will remain the framework for Hegel's political and social thought, even after its defeat. Kojève therefore quite properly takes the next step and as it were writes a new last chapter in the historical series: this is the condition in which Napoleon (or Stalin, depending on how we read Kojève's code words), the Master of the World, is reflected in the equality of the Napoleonic citizens, who are the "synthesis of the Master-warrior and the Slave-worker. What is new in this state is that everyone is (from time to time) warrior (conscription) and all participate in social labor" (146). Meanwhile this now fully human condition will result in the supreme value of the Kojèvian ethos, that of *Befriedigung* or satisfaction: the enjoyment of absolute collective self-consciousness or of a fully human and transparent world. The figure of Napoleon then generates yet another shape or subject; it is that of Hegel himself or the Sage.

> To be sure, only the head of the universal and homogenous state (Napoleon) is really "satisfied" (that is to say, recognized by all in his personal reality and value). He alone is therefore truly free (more than all the heads of state before him, who were always "limited" by the "specific differences" of all families, classes and nations). But all citizens are here potentially "satisfied," for each one can become this head or chief, whose personal ("particular") action is at one and the same time a "universal" act (an act of state), or in other words the doing of all (*das Tun Aller und Jedes*). For there is no longer any heredity (as "non-human," "natural," "pagan" element). Each can therefore actualize his Desire for recognition: on condition he accepts (element of Mastery) the risk of death competition implies in this State (political struggle—a risk that in any case guarantees the "*sérieux*" of the candidates); and also on condition he has previously taken part in Society's activities of construction, in a collective Labor which maintains the State in its existence and reality (element of servitude and service, which also guarantees the "competence" of the candidates). The "satisfaction" of the Citizen is thus a result of the synthesis in him of the Master-warrior and the Slave-worker. So what is new in this State is that everyone in it is from time to time a warrior (universal conscription) and that everyone also participates in social labor. As for the Sage (Hegel), he limits himself to Understanding: the State and its Chief, the Citizen, both warrior and worker, and finally himself (by way of the *Phenomenology*, at the conclusion of which he encounters himself as the result, the final end and integration of the historical process of humanity). This sage, who reveals (by "Knowledge") reality (as incarnated in Napoleon), is the incarnation of Absolute Spirit: he is thus, if you like, the incarnate God of whom the Christians dreamt (the real or veritable Christ = Napoleon-Jesus + Hegel-Logos; incarnation therefore takes place, not in the middle but at the very end of historical time). (*ILH*, 146–7, translation mine).

Such is Kojève's narrativization of Absolute Spirit; it has the merit of grounding the possibility of knowing the social totality in its post-revolutionary preconditions and of adding an historical context to what might only bewilderingly come before us as a disembodied form of pure thought. I have, however, already suggested that it is no longer satisfying to anthropomorphize the "notion" of Absolute Spirit, to make it into a character whose appearance marks the end of an historical narrative.

Yet I now want to argue that despite the enrichment of the Hegelian problematic which we owe to Kojève, his rewriting of the *Phenomenology* falls back behind Hegel's own narrative in significant ways.

For one thing, the dialectical structure of his "universal and homogenous state" replicates Hegel's dialectic of the Roman Empire (as I hinted above). It confronts us with an opposition between the unique subjectivity of the Emperor (this time Napoleon) and those—equal yet without his essential "satisfaction"—of the masses as such. Kojève wrote indeed in the period of the "long Cold War," in which such charismatic figures, from Stalin to de Gaulle, from Hitler to F. D. R., played a more than significant role: a period which seems to have come to an end with the end of the post-war period (or the advent of postmodernity and late capitalism). For one thing, it is important for contemporary readers not to confuse the celebrity status with which we are familiar today with the operative meaning of Weberian charisma, which is rather different from the appeal of an attractive personality or even the power of a personality as such. Stalin, however interesting for us, does not seem to have been blessed with the kind of personality that radiates fascination; while Hitler's power was that of the spellbinding orator rather than of character as such. Indeed, we must affirm, against Kojève, that true charisma includes the power of the Sage and is inseparable from it: for what Kojève calls the Sage can essentially be described in Lacanian terms as the Big Other itself, the "subject supposed to know," the locus of a wisdom and authority structurally unavailable to the masses of equal subjects who are also, in principle, equal to Him.

Meanwhile, in a second moment of this argument, we must now assert that the days of the Big Other are over, a proposition empirically verifiable in world leaders everywhere, but which has its ground in the spirit of the age more generally, which can be characterized as that of Cynical Reason, whose existence is rather to be accounted for on the other side of Kojève's opposition, namely the historically new condition of his post-revolutionary population.

For the kernel of truth of Kojève's "end of history" is essentially to be found on the social level, rather than on that political level which his terminology of a "universal empire" seems to suggest. The convergence he implicitly posits between the US and the Soviet Union is not a political one: It is that of the social equality of societies which have swept traditional class culture away (or have never known it in the first place). In European class culture, the triumphant bourgeoisie, while displacing the old aristocracy, borrows the very structure and dynamic of the latter's culture, and perpetuates the latter's hierarchies in new forms and with new content. Post-revolutionary society, however—and today we can certainly include China along with the Soviet Union in that category—has by a process of violent leveling destroyed the very social structures of class culture; while, by virtue of the absence of feudalism and the accumulation of immigrants (as well as the standardizing effects of mass culture), the United States has also escaped both the European class structures and those of non-European (pre-modern) caste societies.

But it is important to understand this process socially and culturally, rather than economically. The prodigious social leveling which is identified here certainly does not exclude the emergence of wealth and of profound distinctions between rich and poor, even in the socialist countries. Nor is it in any way to be understood as the end of classes in their economic sense: there are still workers and managers in these societies, there is still profit and exploitation, reserve armies of the unemployed, and so on and so forth. But the new cultural equality—I would prefer to characterize it as plebeianization—is infused with a powerful hatred of hierarchy and special privileges and with a passionate resentment of caste distinctions and inherited cultural superiority. It is permitted to be wealthy, as long as the rich man is as vulgar as everyone else: this universal democratic impulse is negative rather than positive, it is fired by a passion for egalitarianism which is not quite the same as the ressentiment against success (although it can easily degenerate into that) and which is akin to the older revolutionary mob spirit without being revolutionary—insofar as all these equals have in principle achieved what Kojève calls "satisfaction," which is as he significantly notes itself quite different from "happiness" (149).

Kojève's achievement is thus paradoxically to have described the waning of that Master/Slave dialectic which he was credited with reviving in modern philosophy. In terms of power, for example, the place of the absent Master ("qui est allé," perhaps, "puiser les pleurs du Styx"), great multinational corporations now deploy the investments of worldwide capital, themselves enjoying the twin status of personification on the legal level (the soulful corporation), while on that of the social imaginary or political unconscious they become more and more difficult to visualize or to represent. But I believe that Hegel is here more advanced than Kojève and has more productive clues to offer as to the continuing significance of that "recognition" which Kojève restricted to the interpersonal struggle between Master and Slave.

We must therefore retrace our steps and reread Hegel's account of post-revolutionary consciousness, while historicizing that final moment—morality after Kant, the autonomy of the citizen—which traditional readers have also read as an end of history—the achievement of freedom and democracy—albeit as a rather different kind of end of history—a bourgeois one—than the plebeianization of Kojève's universal state.

A number of categorical oppositions need to be taken into account here, even though it will only be a question here of adding an economic dialectic to Hegel's essentially political one (both of them mobilizing Kojève's new population of social subjects). But, perhaps, insofar as the political is the affair of the Masters and the economic the production of the Slaves or workers, this reduplication and parallelism itself remains faithful to Kojève's initial insight.

At any rate, it will be necessary to play these developments out along several axes. We recall that in the older religious dialectic, in which Rome is opposed to Christianity, what counted was a dialectic of the abstract and the concrete. The Roman emperor was the locus of subjectivity, the uniquely concrete individual in a world of empty or abstract juridical equality: the concrete subjectivity of an inner Christianity then answers the needs of that population, giving it content at the same time that the Emperor's subjectivity was revealed to be empty and abstract. (The same dialectic was however repeated within the "Unhappy Consciousness" of Christianity, in which the uniquely concrete and individual subjectivity is other and elsewhere for its empty subjects, longing for their individual fulfillment and salvation.)

Alongside this opposition of the abstract and the concrete, we must identify another one, which is registered in the sequence of Hegel's chapters, namely the collective ("revolutionary terror") and the individual ("morality"). The Roman emperor (not to speak of the Napoleon of Kojève) is not finally able to stand as a synthesis of these two dimensions of social life. Rousseau's General Will stands as another, more desperate and more ingenious attempt, to put these categories back together in such a way that the "complex term" is not a personification or an anthropomorphic figure of any kind, and yet somehow enacts the collectivity of the social in a fashion that excludes majorities, pluralities or even unanimities—that, in other words, evades the quantitative altogether. It is thus the revolutionary subject, or better still, the Fichtean-Lukacsean subject-object of history, provided (once again) we are able to neutralize the irresistible slippage of the concept and of the word "subject" towards individual subjectivity and anthropomorphism.

Unfortunately this is impossible, and even seen as an event rather than a concept—the event of this axial revolution itself—the General Will slips fatally into abstraction, and lethal abstraction at that. According to the letter of Hegel's text then (rather than following Kojève's insertion of the Napoleonic universal state), the failure of the collective, of the General Will and its revolution, is followed by what looks like a restoration of the individual and its subjectivity, now, since Kant, reorganized in terms of personal morality. Indeed, the Kantian "categorical imperative" is also meant to be a new and original reunification of individual and collective, insofar as it enjoins us to grasp our individual acts as universal laws. Politically, the Kantian ethic is supposed to project the new autonomous subjectivity of the citizen (and politically to correspond to the great project of the age, from the American Revolution onwards, which is the framing of a written constitution).

Yet the Restoration did not exactly turn out as Hegel anticipated, and we will posit the failure of this post-revolutionary subject just as surely as that of the revolutionary one: neither the General Will nor the categorical imperative effectuate that reconciliation of the individual-subjective and the universal-collective which, if achieved, would presumably spell the end of history as such (or, if you prefer Marx's formulation, the end of pre-history!). But failure here means simply that Kantian morality (like the revolution of the General Will, along with its prior conceptualization or theorization by Rousseau) is now to be taken as an historical event; or, to keep to the spirit of Hegel's experience of history, as a determinate contradiction, one which brings new problems and new contradictions into actuality along with it.

Yet Hegel does introduce a wholly new element at the end of this chapter, which I will consider to be the end of Hegel's narrative, broken off in mid-course by History itself (and to which the supplementary non-narrative chapters on religion and Absolute Spirit have been added, as though in afterthought). This is a new and heightened kind of recognition which will now open up two new and parallel outcomes for the *Phenomenology*'s historical narrative, on the side of the subject and of the object respectively, outcomes which are hardly to be read as the endings of history either, but which break off at the present of our own time as Hegel's did at his.

I.

A new note is indeed struck by the Dostoyevskian scene of guilt and confession that appears to be meant to bring the Kantian ethic of the *Sollen* or ethical obligation up to date: not only to reintroduce genuine subjectivity and feeling into the notoriously dry and abstract world of Kantian duty, but also, in a more fundamental way, to replace obligation with immanence, and the infinite futurity of duty with the already fulfilled satisfaction of activity. It is at this point that Hegel seems to me to revise and transform his earlier version of "recognition" and to move considerably beyond what Kojève so insightfully brought to our attention in Hegel's earlier chapters.

What is at stake, indeed, is the individual's recognition of his responsibility for the law, something rather different than his responsibility to the law or before the law, yet which includes both those nuances.

This is a complex variation on the idealist or "speculative" identification of subject with object, and bears very decisively on the whole question of alienation and transparency as those play themselves out in the social and political spheres. For the solution brought by the tradition of German idealist philosophy from Kant on to the problem of citizenship and obedience involves the acknowledgement of the seemingly external laws (including the constitution) as something I myself have brought into being to which I am therefore bound by an identification much more intense than rational choice or freedom. I have myself produced the law, and therefore it is not alien to me, it belongs to me and there can thus be no question of my disobedience. This is, to be sure, a very different theory of the claims of legal authority than any contractual theories of society; and it is clearly at work in that Dostoyevskian dialectic of conscience and guilt which we have so surprisingly found at work in Hegel's account of modern individualistic ethics, where the acknowledgement of guilt now turns out to be the familiar discovery by the Hegelian subject of its profound kinship and even oneness with the object. Nor is the word transparency out of place here insofar as it signifies my reconciliation with the social order and my discovery and acceptance of my own complicity with it.

Now to be sure this particular theory of legal obligation has its grim side, insofar as it seems to require, not merely a confession of guilt, but a consent to punishment, on the part of the criminal, seen now, not as a rebel against an alien order, but an unhappy consciousness divided against itself and caught between its own illusions about its private or subjective desires and acts and that other self in fact unconsciously embodied in the law it has itself transgressed. The monstrous shadows thrown by such a position are to be observed in Kleist's *Michael Kohlhaas*, or in the following terrible remark by Kant:

> Even if civil society were to dissolve itself, with the consent of all its members (for example, if a people who inhabited an island decided to separate and to disperse to other parts of the world), the last murderer in prison would first have to be executed in order that each should receive his deserts and that the people should not bear the guilt of a capital crime through failing to insist on its punishment . . .[36]

It is against this well-nigh inhuman rigor that Hegel's evocation of pardon and redemption is set: yet we must understand this in a more fundamental framework, namely that of the individual's recognition that he is himself the author of the social and legal fabric that seems to condemn him; in other words, that this seemingly alien institution of the Law is his own making, well in advance of any individual admission of culpability, any purely individual repentance or expression of regret for the act and guilt before society. This is then a wholly new sense of recognition: not that of the enigmatic other as a human like myself or an embodiment of the same freedom as which I know myself; but rather a recognition of myself in the object world and its social institutions, a recognition of these as my own constructions, as the only temporarily alienated embodiments of my own activity.

For what looked before like the purely anti-social or sociopathological act—crime, or crime as considered from a bourgeois ethical perspective, an aberrant refusal of the social order and the gratuitous violence of a sick and isolated individual—now as ethics slowly turns into the institution of bourgeois law and confession seals the acknowledgement of my own responsibility for the very construction and production of the social in the first place (what I will call

---

[36] Immanuel Kant, "Metaphysics of Morals," in *Kant's Political Writings*, ed. Hans Reiss, Cambridge: Cambridge University Press, 1970, 156.

a Sartrean "assumption" or recognition or reappropriation of the hitherto alienated social order). Such reassumption then slowly turns back into the political protest of the individuals against that alienation and a form of revolt that seeks to prolong the revolutionary transformation of society into the reappropriation of its alienated institutions by a radical democratization and plebeianization. What lies beyond the horizon of this reassumption of the social and the political is the human age itself—the fully human and humanly produced world—and the end of alienation and external forms of power and domination.

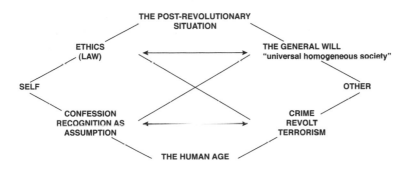

2.

Yet this is as it were only the subjective form taken by the prolongation of the Hegelian dialectic into modernity: we must also identify the objective form of this process, something suggested by a different feature of the dialectic of recognition, namely the labor on matter performed by the Slave. When we recall the rereading that has been proposed above of the post-Kantian ethic—the way in which the individual is called upon to acknowledge the law as his own production—we may begin to see that a whole logic of production emerges here on the objective side of the modern contradiction, and also that it differs from the Roman/Christian moment insofar as it is the production of a whole world. Just as the modern dialectic on the one hand foregrounded a subjective opposition between universal abstract freedom and an equally universal private life, so here we now find two worlds opposed to each other at the same time that they are little more than two dimensions or faces of the same (now global) historical moment. One of these has to do with the world of objects produced by the Slave and his modern equivalents, the other has to do with the humanization of that world and its de-naturalization, that is to say, with our recognition of that entire post-natural world as the product of human praxis and production.

The object world confronted by the post-revolutionary subject is indeed here evoked by Hegel in the most startling and unexpected fashion: it is the world of utilitarianism, which is by no means judged as negatively as one might expect in the context of Hegelian ideal-ism, even though a certain unassimilability of that world of objects is also stressed. For alongside that "empty husk of pure being" which is posited by the unity of deism (or of the surviving religious remnant)—the world of content, of individual things or what Heidegger would call the ontic, or *Seiendes*—that object-world, even though it "places itself outside of that unity, is an alternation—an alternation which does not return into itself, an alternation of being-for-an-other, and of being-for-self; it is reality in the way this is an object for the actual consciousness of pure insight—Utility" (428/353). The alternation theorized by Hegel here indeed foreshadows that between produc-tion and consumption in the commodity form, a combination itself underscored by an even more explicit rehearsal of the process.

> Both ways of viewing the positive and the negative relations of the finite to the in-itself are, however, in fact equally necessary, and everything is thus as much something *in itself* as it is *for an "other"*; in other words, everything is *useful*. Everything is at the mercy of everything else, now lets itself be used by others and is *for them*, and now, so to speak, stands again on its hind legs, is stand-offish towards the other, is for itself, and uses the other in its turn. From this, we see what is the essence and the place of man regarded as a Thing that is *conscious* of this relation. As he immediately is, as a natural consciousness *per se*, man is good, as an individual he is absolute and all else exists for him; and moreover, since the moments have for him, *qua* self-conscious animal, the significance of

universality, *everything* exists for his pleasure and delight and, as one who has come from the hand of God, he walks the earth as in a garden planted for him. He must also have plucked the fruit of the tree of the knowledge of Good and Evil. He possesses in this an advantage which distinguishes him from all other creatures, for it happens that his intrinsically good nature is *also* so constituted that an excess of pleasure does it harm, or rather his individuality has *also its beyond* within it, can go beyond itself and destroy itself. To counter this, Reason is for him a useful instrument for keeping this excess within bounds, or rather for preserving himself when he oversteps his limit; for, this is the power of consciousness. Enjoyment on the part of the conscious, intrinsically *universal* being, must not itself be something determinate as regards variety and duration, but universal. "Measure" or proportion has therefore the function of preventing pleasure in its variety and duration from being cut short; i.e. the function of "measure" is immoderation. Just as everything is useful to man, so man is useful too, and his vocation is to make himself a member of the group, of use for the common good and serviceable to all. The extent to which he looks after his own interests must also be matched by the extent to which he serves others, and so far as he serves others, so far is he taking care of himself: one hand washes the other. But wherever he finds himself, there he is in his right place; he makes use of others and is himself made use of. (342–343)

Beide Betrachtungsweisen, der positiven wie der negativen Beziehung des Endlichen auf das Ansich, sind aber in der Tat gleich notwendig, und alles ist also so sehr *an sich,* als es *für ein Anderes* ist, oder alles ist *nützlich.*—Alles gibt sich anderen preis, läßt sich jetzt von anderen gebrauchen und ist *für sie;* und jetzt stellt es *sich,* es so zu sagen, wieder auf die Hinterbeine, tut spröde gegen Anderes, ist für sich und gebraucht das Andere seinerseits.—Für den Menschen, als das dieser Beziehung *bewußte* Ding, ergibt sich daraus sein Wesen und seine Stellung. Er ist, wie er unmittelbar ist, als natürliches Bewußtsein *an sich, gut,* als Einzelnes *absolut,* und Anderes ist *für ihn;* und zwar, da für ihn als das seiner bewußte Tier die Momente die Bedeutung der Allgemeinheit haben, ist *alles* für sein Vergnügen und Ergötzlichkeit, und er geht, wie er aus Gottes Hand gekommen, in der Welt als einem für ihn gepflanzten Garten umher.—Er muß auch vom Baume der Erkenntnis des Guten und des Bösen gepflückt haben; er besitzt darin einen Nutzen, der ihn von allem anderen unterscheidet, denn zufälligerweise ist seine an sich gute Natur *auch* so beschaffen, daß ihr das Übermaß der Ergötzlichkeit Schaden tut, oder vielmehr seine Einzelheit hat *auch ihr Jenseits* an ihr, kann über sich selbst hin-ausgehen und sich zerstören. Hiergegen ist ihm die Vernunft ein nützliches Mittel, dies Hinausgehen gehörig zu beschränken oder vielmehr im Hinausgehen über das Bestimmte sich selbst zu erhalten; denn dies ist die Kraft des Bewußtseins. Der Genuß des bewußten an sich *allgemeinen* Wesens muß nach Mannigfaltigkeit und Dauer selbst nicht ein Bestimmtes, sondern allgemein sein; das Maß hat daher die Bestimmung, zu verhindern, daß das Vergnügen in seiner Mannigfaltigkeit und Dauer abgebrochen werde; d. h. die Bestimmung des Maßes ist die Unmäßigkeit.—Wie dem Menschen alles nützlich ist, so ist er es ebenfalls und seine Bestimmung eben so sehr, sich zum gemeinnützlichen und allgemein brauchbaren Mitgliede des Trupps zu machen. Soviel er für sich sorgt, gerade soviel muß er *sich auch* hergeben für die anderen, und soviel er sich hergibt, soviel sorgt er für sich selbst; eine Hand wäscht die andere. Wo er aber sich befindet, ist er recht daran; er nützt anderen und wird genützt. (415–416)

It is worth insisting for another moment on the positive dimension of this process of humanization, which to be sure leaves the inhabit-ants of its world vulnerable to objectification and instrumentalization, to themselves being treated as means rather than ends. This negative possibility constituted the very source of Kantian ethics and expressed the general distaste of the German philosophers, very much including Hegel, for England as a "nation of shopkeepers," as the very heartland of utilitarianism and commercialism. But the valences of the dialec-tic demand the registering of both positive and negative dimensions of a given phenomenon simultaneously, and are therefore necessarily distinct from moralizing critiques and judgments.

Meanwhile what Hegel calls utility is prophetic of the Hedeggerian being-in-the-world and can assuredly be translated into what has been called Heidegger's "pragmatism." Heidegger showed, indeed, that "utility," which he calls *Zuhandenheit* (or ready-to-hand-ness), is the most immediate or primary dimension of the being of things and their constitution into a world, and not some mere human addition to nature as such, an erroneous concept he attributes to epistemology or to the more derivative experience of things as "*vorhanden*" or merely present in inert, contemplative fashion.

There can to be sure be other objections to the celebration of a full humanization of the world and an end or subsumption of nature (it is indeed in this way that postmodernity has often been characterized); but we will come to them at the end of the present discussion.

We must now dialectically identify this modern utilitarian world of objects confronted by post-revolutionary experience with its subjective analogue in post-Kantian ethics. For as we began to show above, it is the trace of production itself which characterized that ethics, and it is the recognition of that production in the objective world, the acknowledgement of my own activity in its social and material construction, that constitutes me as a citizen. Here, to be sure, the focus tends to shift from the object world of utility to the social world of the state and of laws: yet Hegel's originality in his proposal for a post-Kantian ethics is to have reoriented the emphasis from obedience to the law and the state to the very production of these collective institutions. This feeling of collective property rather than individual property, of collective ownership rather than narrowly personal possession, is in Hegel's philosophy of activity and *Tätigkeit* the very source of my identification with the post-revolutionary (Utopian) society; and Kojève is right in identifying this participation as a far deeper satisfaction (*Befriedigung*) than mere consumption or abstract legal title. Indeed, we can form a more concretely overdetermined view of this new object world—both as utilitarian or *zuhanden* and as my externalization or the output of my own production—by bringing to light all the subterranean relationships that bind these themes to the phenomenon of the *Sache selbst* discussed above. In the non-abstractable recognition of the experience of "the thing itself"—my acknowledgement of my vocation, of my deeper calling within the varieties of activity—there lies implicit the identification of the work as my own production as well as that recognition by other people of the usefulness of my labor for them, or in other words a universality which cannot be theorized or philosophized but exists at the level of that world of singular objects which is daily life.

It is precisely this kind of identification which the former slave—now become ethical citizen—will ideally bring to the externalized object in which the subject is to see itself. And this is the deeper truth of the idea that the law will be acknowledged by virtue of the citizen's production of it: the revolutionary state is itself the construction and the achievement, the production, of its citizens, and that is the moral sense in which it belongs to them and in which obeying its laws is tantamount to obeying themselves. Political apathy, meanwhile, expresses the well-nigh literal alienation of the state, which still belongs to others and has nothing to do with me.

It is thus scarcely a distortion to posit the humanized world of consumer society as that externalization in which the subject can find itself most completely objectified and yet most completely itself. The contradiction begins to appear when we set this cultural dimension alongside the legal and political levels of late capitalism: for it is with these that the Kantian ethical citizen ought to identify himself, according to the theory, and in these that he ought to be able to recognize his own subjectivity and the traces of his own production. But this is precisely what does not obtain today, where so many people feel powerless in the face of the objective institutions which constitute their world, and in which they are so far from identifying that legal and political world as their own doing and their own production. Here, despite the historical fact of production itself—the human world, which, as Vico put it, people have themselves produced—we find universal alienation of the most literal kind, in which the object, the not-I, comes before its subjects as what is radically other and the property and dominion of a foreign power.

"Just as man is governed, in religion, by the products of his own brain, so, in capitalist production, he is governed by the products of his own hand."[37] Indeed, it is not sufficiently recognized that Marx's

---

[37] Karl Marx, *Capital*, vol. 1, trans. Ben Fowkes, London: Penguin, 1976.

early philosophical theory of alienation (which remains a structural principle in *Capital* at moments like this one) includes within its account of expropriation the more positive Hegelian demonstration that such externalized and alienated objects continue to belong to the worker in all senses of that word.

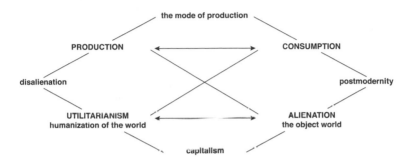

On the basis of Hegel's transformation of his concept of recognition into that of the disalienation of a human age estranged from us and expressed in the religious language of acknowledgement and redemption to be found on the concluding page of his morality chapter, a page which on our reading concludes the *Phenomenology* as such—we have constructed a later stage which remains a provisional one and by no means an historically final moment or "end of history." This provisional halt, which corresponds to Hegel's own historical present, was then structured in the form of a double opposition or contradiction: an immense dialectical confrontation between the modern subject and its humanized object world. On the one hand the modern subject is divided into abstract equality and richly private or existential individuality; on the other hand, a utilitarian world of objects confronts the alienated reality of the subject's production of the object world and of post-revolutionary secular society as such. This model of contradiction is no anachronistic superposition of contemporary themes and anxieties on an old-fashioned Hegelian system, but has been constituted by a rearrangement of features and analyses already present in Hegel's chapters on contemporary history. (A word on contradiction itself: we have here taken as a model the very structural logic of the *Antigone* chapter discussed earlier. The historically new opposition that emerged here between human and divine law, between the state and the clan, was not only a prophetic symptom of the dissolution of the social form it tore apart, but was also the very foundational moment of that social form in the first place. The polis was only able to come into being as a political form and a mode of production by virtue of the articulation of this constitutive opposition which ended up destroying it.)

It may now be appropriate to project a further play of opposites that takes these twin dialectics of subject and object speculatively into some far future of social revolution and ecological transformation:

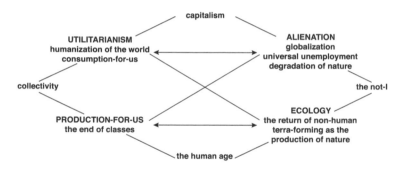

This is then what must also be said about the fundamental contradiction of modernity which has been outlined here. The articulation into its two dimensions of subjectivity and object world inaugurates modern society at the same time that it condemns it to dissolution. The contradiction signals the failure of the social system, provided one understands that in that sense all social systems are failures. As Slavoj Žižek puts it: "does not Hegel's *Phenomenology* tell us again and again the same story of the repeated failure, of the subject's endeavor to realize his project in social substance?"[38] Yet from another perspective what is crucial about contradiction is that its very emergence signals the interiorization of the opposites, which no longer confront each

---

[38] See note 13 above.

other in external and contingent ways. This interiorization might then be grasped as a kind of historical progress from Hegel's perspective, although it is surely to be understood as a structural rather than a teleological (let alone a cyclical) movement.

I propose that, with the hindsight of Marx's dialectic in *Capital,* we understand this progression in the sense of enlargement, as of a spiral rather than of a circular or cyclical process. We have already posited the essence of the Hegelian "universal" as the presence to and within the subject of other people: what then is more predictable, at least in our earthly human history, than the progressive enlargement of that population of others to be included in the fateful philosophical world? It is indeed a commonplace of historiography from well before Hegel's own philosophy of history that the failure of the Greek city-states (the drama of *Antigone*) is predicated on their spatial limits and their resultant multiplicity, and that they are overcome by the enlargement of a single city-state into an empire, and its subsequent unification of the ancient world. For unity is the other constant in this process, and the unity and dimensions of the (revolutionary) nation-state are in this sense a further progression. Hegel's system itself thereby calls in its very structure for the subsequent enlargements of later history: first the moment of imperialism (or the "modern" in the technical sense) and now that of globalization. These subsequent enlargements are very much in the spirit of the Hegelian dialectic and also explain why Hegel's own practice is no longer to be associated with dilemmas of "modernity" as Pippin would have it, but must now be reconjugated in terms of a world market that is only in the process of finding and inventing the conceptuality appropriate to it.

Chapter 10

Religion as Cultural Superstructure

Yet the *Phenomenology* does not conclude with the chapter on "morality" which we have reinserted into a somewhat different narrative conclusion: there remain two further chapters, "Religion"—virtually a treatise in itself—and "Absolute Spirit"—a most sketchy and disappointing anticlimactic conclusion for so intricate a work. So far we have dealt with neither one, but I have a few proposals for doing so. Hegel is himself aware of the paradoxical nature of his return to the topic of religion here, after its various more purely historical or structural appearances in the earlier chapters, in Unhappy Consciousness (early Christianity), or the struggle between Belief and Enlightenment. As with the other problems posed by the organization of the *Phenomenology*, external motives and authorial intentions are not satisfactory in explaining this enormous supplement, which we must account for by the supposition that the author felt something to be missing from his previous narrative, despite its chronological completion in the modern times of the 1807 writing. What is missing is then added by the narrative reduplication of everything that succeeded it, so that we have to go back in time, even earlier than the Greco-Roman period, in order to grasp the first rudimentary forms of religion in a prehistoric past which cannot even be supposed to correlate with the mythic time of the Master/Slave encounter.

It should be added that this new narrative more or less coincides with the structural narrative of the *Äesthetik*: first, the primacy of matter over spirit (what Hegel calls the sublime, as in the pyramids); second, their anthropomorphic equilibrium, as in classical Greek sculpture; finally, the primacy of spirit over matter, as in the language arts, or in another way, Christianity. This third (or Romantic) stage then proves to be in competition with philosophy, which would seem more fully and self-consciously, in the Notion, to achieve what literature vainly attempts in the projects of romanticism or what theology projects as the Trinity. At this point, a new distinction is underscored between the picture-thinking of art or religion and the philosophical Notion (*Begriff*) as such. This conflation of the dynamic of religion with that of aesthetics is very significant indeed, and we will return to it shortly.

For the moment, what is indispensable is to bracket everything we traditionally associate with religion and to approach this topic as though it were utterly unfamiliar to us, as a Martian might approach human mental functions for which it has no equivalent. Let us assume, then, that Hegel is not theorizing this matter whose name we know already, and with which we are (closely or distantly) associated in daily life (people going to church, confessional adherence, rituals and devotional lip-service) or at least recognize from a reading of history. The new interpretation will require us to deduce from Hegel's text what might be the object of his thinking in this chapter, or in other words what might for us be the equivalent of such an object in a postmodern world in which "religion" is merely the word for neo-ethnic group narcissisms, incomprehensible fanaticism, or one specific public language or code among others.

I would suggest, then, that such an investigation will find itself pursuing three specific features: the seeming autonomy (or semi-autonomy) of this strange object; the nature of its thought-mode, namely *Vorstellung*, generally and most suggestively translated as "picture-thinking"; and finally the problem of allegory. The kinship with art, whose consequences we have not yet fully explored, extends through each of these features.

Thus, for example, that seeming autonomy of what Hegel calls religion, which dictates its separate treatment in what is a virtually self-complete chapter (and later on a whole separate seminar or lecture series), is certainly echoed by the self-completeness of Hegel's later aesthetic lectures. Here, in the *Phenomenology*, however, the opposite process would seem to be taking place, the Religion chapter almost completely absorbing questions of art and aesthetics in such a way that they receive no independent treatment in their own right. Yet a kind of compromise is reached in which classical religion— apparently unacceptable to Hegel in the form of polytheism—finds itself partially replaced and represented by Greek drama and sculpture and by the communal ritual of the mysteries.

There is, then, some structural analogy between the semi-autonomous status of art and that of religion here: both are inner-worldly events or activities within human life which are nonetheless sufficiently external to it to be capable of knowing their own developmental logic and functioning as independent sign-systems, both reflecting the world in some way and able from time to time to intervene in it. This is the paradox Marcuse theorized in "The Affirmative Character of Culture," in which the amphibious status of such levels or forms enabled them to pass from a critical negation of their world to a slavish legitimization of and complicity with it; or rather, dialectically, to perform both functions simultaneously. But this structural ambiguity makes it clear why it is not possible to isolate such objects of study and to produce a systematic philosophy for them: for such philosophical definition already takes sides and endows the object with a positive or negative function that cancels the essential, namely the very ambiguity or "unity of opposites" that gives them their specificity in the first place.

The autonomy of either art or religion is therefore to be found in the very impossibility of specifying their identities as autonomous levels or elements. At the same time both prove to be objects which call for the attention of theory (rather than philosophy) and of the dialectic as just such an approach to the unity of opposites. These are objects which intermittently fade in and out of real life, sometimes identifying with it so closely as to be indistinguishable, sometimes emerging as wholly separate and distinct spheres or practices which have nothing to do with the everyday. But such ambiguities are not to be overcome by precise definitions and conceptual delimitations, but rather constitute structural characteristics around which any thinking of them must centrally and primarily orient itself. The "end" of religion in secularization and modernity will therefore be no less problematic and equivocal than the "end" of art itself (let alone the "end of history," which is a wholly different proposition from either of these). We must therefore see if there exist other such phenomena in the contemporary world to which semi-autonomy of this kind might be attributed.

As for picture-thinking, it is certainly noteworthy to what degree that popular German-idealist or romantic concept called Imagination plays so little a part in Hegel's writing or system; and one is tempted to conjecture that it is precisely the omnipresence of the role of so-called picture-thinking (*Vorstellung*) in Hegel that leaves so little place for it. Picture-thinking would seem for Hegel to have a strong kinship with *Verstand*, or in other words with the common-sense empirical thinking of externality, formed in the experience of solid objects and obedient to the law of non-contradiction. But where Reason (*Vernunft*)—what we may often simply call the dialectic— has the task of transforming the necessary errors of *Verstand* into new and dialectical kinds of truths, its vocation when faced with picture-thinking is somewhat different. If *Verstand* brings with it the errors of empiricism, picture-thinking on the other hand is already an experience of truth, albeit a distorted and preconceptual one. Reason must transcend and transform the errors of *Verstand*, but it must hermeneutically recover the truths of *Vorstellung*, even though the latter have also been formed into images in accordance with the logic of the senses and of externality.

For the idealist then, images are presumably already part of Spirit in ways in which sense-impressions are not (or at least not obviously); or to put it another way, we do not bring to the exercise of picture-thinking the same kind of certainty which accompanies *Verstand*; the former is somehow fictional or imaginary, while the latter is legitimated by reference to external objects. We can convey the difference metaphysically (and in a perhaps less attractive idealistic way) by conceiving both these faculties as entangled in the body and therefore in the sensory: *Verstand* then accepts these limitations and invents its conceptuality and its language on the basis of the physical, while *Vorstellung* attempts to transcend the sensory by means of the sensory, designating itself as necessarily incomplete and unsatisfactory, as the determinate failure to attain the realm of the Notion (or *Begriff*).

To be sure, the translation of *Vorstellung* as picture-thinking is already an interpretation in itself; and it is perhaps not the term that would seem the most appropriate one if one consults *Encyclopedia vol. 3* (Hegel's anthropology, or *Philosophy of Spirit*, paragraph 451 and thereafter), where Wallace and Miller render the German as "representation." But if one examines the discussion, in the *Lectures on the Philosophy of Religion*, of what is surely the paradigmatic form of *Vorstellung* in Hegel's system, namely the Trinity, the pictorial dimension of such thought is inescapable, particularly insofar as so much of Hegel's early writings are concerned with this theological concept: indeed, the formal similarities of the tripartite dialectic with the theological interpretation of the Trinity have led many interpreters either to locate the origins of the dialectic in these theological reflections or else to pronounce Hegel a Christian thinker without further ado.

But such similarities, and the differences they also necessarily entail, will be very useful indeed in establishing the relationship of such picture-thinking to what Hegel characterizes as the truly philosophical thinking of the *Begriff* or Notion, which mere abstraction is perhaps too poor a term to convey. It is certain that Hegel's theorization of this relationship is rather shaky: we cannot appreciate what is meant by "filling" (*Stoff*) in the following passage, for example, without wondering whether it is not itself picture-thinking:

> But as religion here is, to begin, *immediate*, this distinction has not yet returned into Spirit. What is posited is only the *Notion of religion*; in this the essence is self-consciousness, which is conscious of being all truth and contains all reality within that truth. This self-consciousness has, as consciousness, *itself for object*. Spirit which, to begin with, has an *immediate* knowledge of itself is thus to itself Spirit in the form of *immediacy*, and the determinateness of the form in which it appears to itself is that

of [mere] *being*. This being, it is true, is *filled* neither with sensation nor a manifold material, nor with any other kind of one-sided moments, purposes, and determinations: it is filled with Spirit and is known by itself to be all truth and reality. Such *filling* is not identical with its *shape*, Spirit *qua* essence is not identical with its consciousness. Spirit is actual as absolute Spirit only when it is also for itself in its *truth* as it is in its *certainty of itself,* or when the extremes into which, as consciousness, it parts itself are explicitly for each other in the shape of Spirit. The shape which Spirit assumes as object of its consciousness remains filled by the certainty of Spirit as by its substance; through this content, the object is saved from being degraded to pure objectivity, to the form of negativity of self-consciousness. Spirit's immediate unity with itself is the basis, or pure consciousness, *within* which consciousness parts asunder [into the duality of subject and object]. In this way Spirit, shut up within its pure self-consciousness, does not exist in religion as the creator of a Nature in general; what it does create in this movement are its *shapes qua* Spirits, which together constitute the completeness of its manifestation. And this movement itself is the genesis of its complete reality through its individual aspects, or through its incomplete shapes. (415–416)

Wie aber hier die Religion erst *unmittelbar* ist, ist dieser Unterschied noch nicht in den Geist- zurückgegangen. Es ist nur der *Begriff* der Religion gesetzt; in diesem ist das Wesen das *Selbstbewußtsein,* das sich alle Wahrheit ist und in dieser alle Wirklichkeit enthält. Dieses Selbstbewußtsein hat als Bewußtsein sich zum Gegenstande; der erst sich *unmittelbar* wissende Geist ist sich also Geist in der *Form* der *Unmittelbarkeit,* und die Bestimmtheit der Gestalt, worin er sich er scheint, ist die des *Seins.* Dies Sein ist zwar weder mit der Empfindung oder dem mannigfaltigen Stoffe noch mit sonstigen einseitigen Momenten, Zwecken und Bestimmungen *erfüllt,* sondern mit dem Geiste und wird von sich als alle Wahrheit und Wirklichkeit gewußt. Diese *Erfüllung* ist auf diese Weise ihrer *Gestalt,* er als Wesen seinem Bewußtsein nicht gleich. Er ist erst als absoluter Geist wirklich, indem er, wie er in *der Gewißheit seiner selbst,* sich auch in seiner *Wahrheit* ist, oder die Extreme, in die er sich als Bewußtsein teilt, in Geistgestalt füreinander sind. Die Gestaltung; welche der Geist als Gegenstand seines Bewußtseins annimmt, bleibt von der Gewißheit des Geistes als von der Substanz erfüllt; durch diesen Inhalt verschwindet dies, daß der Gegenstand zur reinen Gegenständlichkeit, zur Form der Negativität des Selbstbewußtseins herabsänke. Die unmittelbare Einheit des Geistes mit sich selbst ist die Grundlage oder reines Bewußtsein, *innerhalb* dessen das Bewußtsein auseinandertritt. Auf diese Weise in sein reines Selbstbewußtsein eingeschlossen, existiert er in der Religion nicht als der Schöpfer einer *Natur* überhaupt; sondern was er in dieser Bewegung hervorbringt, sind seine Gestalten als Geister, die zusammen die Vollständigkeit seiner Erscheinung ausmachen, und diese Bewegung selbst ist das Werden seiner vollkommenen Wirklichkeit durch die einzelnen Seiten derselben oder seine unvollkommenen Wirklichkeiten. (501–2)

But the drift is clear enough: picture-thinking is halfway between *Verstand* and *Vernunft*, and somehow marked as such and informed by an upward movement.

> When religion has been raised to the level of picture-thinking (*Vorstellung*), it acquires a polemic cast. Its content is not grasped in sensory intuition nor immediately in picture form, but rather mediately, on the way to abstraction, and the sensory or pictorial has been lifted (*aufgehoben*) into the general: and this sublation necessarily includes a negative relationship to the pictorial. Yet this negative direction strikes not only the form— such that the difference between intuition and *Vorstellung* would be present in form alone—but also touches content. In intuition idea and mode of representation are so closely connected that both appear as one, and the pictorial as the meaning of an idea so essentially connected with it that it cannot be separated from it. Picture-thinking, however, emerges from the conviction that the absolutely true idea cannot be grasped by way of a picture, indeed that pictorial representation is a limitation of its content; picture-thinking thereby sublates the unity of intuition, destroys the unity of the picture and its meaning, and lifts the latter up for itself.

> Wenn die Religion in die Form der Vorstellung erhoben ist, so hat sie sogleich etwas *Polemisches* an sich. Der Inhalt wird nicht im sinnlichen Anschauen, nicht auf bildliche Weise unmittelbar aufgefaßt, sondern *mittelbar* auf dem Wege der *Abstraktion,* und das Sinnliche, Bildliche wird in das Allgemeine erhoben; und mit dieser Erhebung ist dann

notwendig das negative Verhalten zum Bildlichen verknüpft. Diese negative Richtung betrifft aber nicht nur die Form, so daß nur in dieser der Unterschied der Anschauung und Vorstellung läge, sondern sie berührt auch den *Inhalt*. Für die Anschauung hängt die *Idee* und die *Weise der Darstellung so* eng zusammen, daß beides als *Eins* erscheint, und das Bildliche hat die Bedeutung, daß die Idee an dasselbe wesentlich geknüpft und von ihm nicht getrennt werden könne. Die Vorstellung hingegen geht davon aus, daß die absolut wahrhafte Idee durch ein Bild nicht gefaßt werden könne und die bildliche Weise eine Beschränkung des Inhalts sei; sie hebt daher jene Einheit der Anschauung auf, verwirft die Einigkeit des Bildes und seiner Bedeutung und hebt diese für sich heraus.[39]

It will not be necessary, particularly in an essay aiming to displace the older schema of the tripartite movement in Hegel with an account of other rhythms, to dwell laboriously on its two-fold role in the Religion chapters: in the Trinity God is the universal, Christ the particular, and the Holy Spirit the individual; while in Hegel's overall developmental scheme of religious history, the premodern sublime is the universal, Greek anthropomorphism the particular, and the Christian or Trinitarian religion the individual.

We are, however, here more interested in the relationship of these religious figures to *Vernunft*, or formally philosophical thinking; and we must admit that—owing as much as anything else to political considerations, to prudence and self-censorship—Hegel's practical implication is ambiguous and it is not clear whether religion is meant to live on after the inauguration of speculative thought, and to coexist with it like a kind of figural accompaniment or indeed a pedagogical propaedeutic; or whether, like the infamous "end of art," it will at that point also have served its purpose and may be allowed to die out altogether. (The question also includes the issue of esoteric versus exoteric doctrine raised in Hegel's introduction.)

At any rate it would seem that the transition out of picture-thinking

---

[39] Hegel, "die Vorstellung," in *Vorlesungen über die Philosophie der Religion* (1821), in *Werke*, vol. 16, 139–140 (English translation mine).

involves the intervention of our old friend production, in a way both reminiscent of Vico (the verum-factum) and anticipatory of the contemporary aesthetic (for which reification is defined as the removal of traces of production from the product). Hegel asserts in this context that,

> what is thought of ceases to be something [merely] thought of, something alien to the self's knowledge, only when the self has produced it, and therefore beholds the determination of the object as its own. (504; 417)

> Denn das Vorgestellte hört nur dadurch auf, Vorgestelltes und seinem Wissen fremd zu sein, daß das Selbst es hervorgebracht hat und also die Bestimmung des Gegenstandes als die *seinige*, somit sich in ihm anschaut. (504)

It is an idea which is not without its dangers for Christianity, even of the Lutheran or inward-feeling/pietistic kind; but also not without its philosophical and literary-critical problems as well, inasmuch as even the bracketing of the old ideas of authorial intention may not be enough to render our picture-thinking fully conscious as a signifying project.

But now it is time to come at all this from the vantage point of contemporary theories of allegory, which Hegel so largely anticipates in his treatment of religion here and in the *Lectures*, as well as in the *Philosophy of History*. These theories must be briefly summarized as generally entailing two propositions: the first is the radical difference between the structure of allegory and that of the symbol; the second is the repudiation of the old point-by-point reading of allegory, that is to say essentially, of the misconception of personification as allegory's predominant mode: thus, the traditional paradigms of allegory such as *Pilgrim's Progress* would have to be reconceptualized in some new non-anthropomorphic way.

As for the symbol, it has since Coleridge been valorized as the vehicle of unity in representation; and there is no reason to modify this description, provided it is understood that unity may no longer have the same aesthetic value for us today. Unity is indeed one of the features at play in Hegel's own account of picture-thinking, but is even here to be sharply distinguished, as a result, from the process of unification as such.

Picture-thinking (or as it is translated here, representation) "holds all sensible and spiritual content in the mode in which it is taken as isolated in its determinacy . . . In representation . . . the distinct characteristics stand on their own account; they might either belong to a whole or be placed outside one another."[40] We need another term than the Romantic keyword "fragment" to characterize such allegorical "isolation" of its items, and even the free-standing nature of "characteristics . . . belonging to a whole," such as Joyce's bodily organs in *Ulysses*: the parts are not fragments but complete in themselves, and yet marked as parts and as conceptually dependent.

Thinking on the other hand—which it is here better to call the thinking of the Notion, rather than abstract or philosophical thought—emphasizes relationships (sometimes Hegel calls it "necessity," in the way in which such interdependence is grasped and foregrounded). It therefore translates the allegorical item into a relational framework which is not at all that of the "organic" unity of the symbol, but which retains the relational distance of the various terms such that they may continue to be apprehended in their interaction (as in the unity of opposites, the alternation from positive to negative and back). This is then the way in which "thinking" in Hegel's sense does not fuse the "bad" isolations of the allegorical items back into the primal unity of the symbol, but rather continues to mark them as isolated from each other at the same time that it restores the web or network of their interactions.

Contemporary theories of allegory thus grasp this structure as the intersection of two principles: that of the autonomy, or complete isolation and non-dependence of their items (which are in that sense not fragments), and at the same time as the marking of those items as conceptually incomplete, as relational terms in a larger signifying structure. Both of these features are then combined in the

---

[40] Ibid., 152–153.

self-designation of allegory as a process rather than any achieved structure or substance. Allegory thus looks back to hallucination as a perceptual isolation of its objects, and forward to the "part-object" as the exemplification of a larger drive that can never be fully satisfied.[41]

It has been pertinently observed that Hegel's various discussions of religion must be seen as a typology rather than a teleological or developmental narrative of some kind[42]; indeed our rather structural reading here of the *Phenomenology* suggests that this approach might helpfully defamiliarize readings of Hegel's texts as a whole, recasting each moment as a determinate variation on subject/object ratios. At any rate the typological structure is clearly visible in the picture-thinking of religion, where all kinds of brilliant readings of the various religions, taken as texts, display Hegel's virtuoso permutations of such ratios. I have elsewhere proposed the example of Indian religious art as a paradigm of such reading, whose structures range from the fetish to the Trinity itself; it is an example about which one need not be defensive in the obvious sense of the limits of the cultural and historical information of Hegel's period (for he himself seems to have known just about everything there was to be known at that date), but which requires a displacement from the usual emphasis on Eurocentrism and even racism (as in the notorious evocation of Africa as a place without history) to just such a structural permutation scheme (in which the identification of this or that religion or culture is relatively indifferent, or opportunistic). Taken in this second way, the Religion chapter is extraordinarily suggestive for contemporary interpretive practices and methods, and will lead us on into a final proposal for the best use of Hegel's ambiguous theory of religion as a semi-autonomous dimension of the social totality.

Indeed, Hegel's notion of religion, in this final substantive chapter of the *Phenomenology*, may be grasped as an attempt to

---

[41] I plan to deal with allegory more extensively in volume 2 of *The Poetics of Social Forms*, entitled *Overtones: The Harmonics of Allegory*.

[42] Peter C. Hodgson, introduction to *Philosophy of Religion: the Lectures of 1827*, by G. W. F. Hegel, ed. Peter C. Hodgson, Berkeley: University of California Press, 1988, 26.

conceptualize, in advance and in the form of a groping historical anticipation, the problematic lineaments of what we call *culture* in our own period, in the broadest anthropological or cultural-studies sense of what organizes daily life and interpolates and forms subjectivities. Indeed, in this sense religion today is itself, in its myriad forms, but the remnants of a cultural system which once governed all the features and contingencies of a simpler social total-ity: a system far more immanent to social relations and production than anything characterized as a superstructure or an ideology in the modern world. The fundamentalisms today express the nostal-gia for such a seemingly more unified world than our own: yet the very possibility of a concept of religion as a distinct entity betrays the inevitable gap or internal distance within the traditional world which such a fantasy conceals or occults.

Nor is the concept of culture foreshadowed by the Hegelian analy-sis of religion to be limited to aesthetics or so-called high culture or high art, although Hegel's theories are suggestive for a reexamina-tion of this more specialized domain of "culture" within the vaster Culture itself. For of his three stages—the Sublime, the Classical and the Romantic—the last two may be seen to project what is today the distinction between Realism—an anthropomorphic or "human-ist" representation of common-sense realities—and Modernism or an often far more intricate reflexive art, in which the very categories of representation are themselves foregrounded and thereby under-mined. As for the moment of the Sublime, it manifests itself in the way in which the sheer physical presence of art and image culture absorbs the mind without a concept, whether in decoration or in a sensory fascination with the raw material of a world and image culture humanly produced.

Still, in modern times, in which art has been differentiated from religion, or from what Benjamin called its cult-value, it has fallen like religion itself to the level of a remnant (albeit a specialized and semi-autonomous survival which, in that also like religion, is capable of making the most overweening claims for itself and its significance). It is therefore in the wider sense of culture as the organization of daily life and of the production of subjectivities designed to function within a specific mode of production, that we must look for the most relevant parallels with Hegel's account.

For with the dedifferentiation of high and low culture, the way in which media culture has seeped into what used to be high literature, while the latter has been displaced as a cultural dominant by the sonorous and the visual if not the spatial itself, culture becomes a rather different term which embraces the totality of society as something like its omnipresent expression, or (using Hegel's word in Hegel's sense) constitutes its spirit. This is the sense in which it is sometimes said that everything is cultural, and that the economic dimension for example, is no longer visible independently, but very much expressed through the very cultural value of its objects as images in either production (work as virtuosity, in Virno[43]) or simply consumption as such.

Leaving aside the theoretical problems involved in assimilating this more general concept of culture to the Marxian notion of the superstructure, we may note a series of features in Hegel's philosophy of religion which are consonant with issues necessarily addressed by modern studies of culture. First of all, there is what we may call the infrastructure specific to such superstructures, namely the existence of institutions and of intellectuals specific to them: a traditional church and priesthood which has in modern times opened up into a variety of intellectual production fields and the specialists who staff them, from the personnel of the advertising and entertainment industries and the academics and journalists concerned with cultural analysis and dissemination to the curators of museums and the government functionaries in charge of cultural budgets, not to speak of the retailers in the art market and analogous networks in the other arts.

It is clear that from this perspective culture today has its performative dimension, something equivalent to Hegel's discussion of the rituals of the religious cult. It has its specific affectivities (or *affects*), which are probably more complex than what Hegel derived as the sheer feeling evoked by contemporary religious ideologists such as

---

[43] Paolo Virno, *A Grammar of the Multitude*, trans. Isabella Bertoletti, James Cascaito, and Andrea Casson, New York: Semiotext[e], 2004.

Schleiermacher. And it has, finally, its own multiple versions of a tension between representationality (or "realism" in the high arts) and reflexivities of all kinds (something analogous to "modernism," but taking any number of distinct forms from self-referential and ironic advertisements and commercials to the more "literary" forms of mass culture).

But it is Hegel's practice of allegorical analysis, in his approach to religious *Vorstellung* or picture-thinking, which is perhaps the most suggestive feature of his philosophy of religion. For here already the conceptual content of what still remains non-abstract and embodied in the various specific material languages of the arts or of narrative is acknowledged and deciphered according to a variety of hermeneutic schemes, which foreshadow ideological analysis as such.

The interrelationship of culture and ideology is very much dialectical in the Hegelian sense, the sense of a kind of "unity of opposites" of representation and meaning, or rather, better still, of the impossibility of thinking either of these dimensions autonomously and in the absence of a dialectical definition of each by the other. It is in this way that the heterogeneity of Hegel's approaches to that he calls religion can stand as an unexpected methodological lesson for contemporary cultural studies, a proposition I will try to elaborate elsewhere.

Chapter 11

Narcissism of the Absolute

Contemporary objections to dialectics in general and to the Hegelian dialectic in particular have been touched on elsewhere.[44] Yet we may as well here register one fundamental source of dissatisfaction aroused by the ideal of the speculative—or the ultimate identity of the subject and object—in Hegel. It is a dissatisfaction which I would prefer, for reasons already discussed above, to dissociate from the question of idealism in whose terms the objection is conventionally formulated.

Narcissism seems to me a better way of identifying what may sometimes be felt to be repulsive in the Hegelian system as such. It is not so much the all-encompassing ambition of the Hegelian philosophical project—sometimes stigmatized as totalization—which is particularly offensive (as the existentialists thought who objected to the reduction of their own individual experience to one moment of the dialectic): for we continue to try to grasp totalities, whether phenomenologically or in some other way, and we continue to try to make connections between the isolated fragments of our thinking and of our experience. Nor is idealism the most telling reproach, if what is in question is merely the translation of the world into consciousness or the Subject (for the existentialists did as much, in their own fashion, nor is the Subject in question necessarily a centered one, as we have tried to show here).

---

[44] See Fredric Jameson, *Valences of the Dialectic*, New York: Verso, 2009, chapter 3.

No, the most serious drawback to the Hegelian system seems to me rather the way in which it conceives of speculative thinking as "the consummation of itself" (namely, of Reason). We have quoted this passage in giving an account of Hegel's critique of epistemology; but perhaps it can now be quoted against himself: Reason, he says there, "must demand that difference, that being, in its manifold variety, become its very own, that it behold itself as the *actual* world and find itself present as a shape and Thing." We thereby search the whole world, and outer space, and end up only touching ourselves, only seeing our own face persist through multitudinous differences and forms of otherness. Never truly to encounter the not-I, to come face to face with radical otherness (or even worse, to find ourselves in an historical dynamic in which it is precisely difference and otherness which is relentlessly being stamped out): such is the dilemma of the Hegelian dialectic, which contemporary philosophies of difference and otherness seem only able to confront with mystical evocations and imperatives. But it is a reproach which may well primarily challenge the Hegelian system as such, rather than the *Phenomenology*, whose heterogeneities we have tried to display here.

Meanwhile, as for Absolute Spirit, it is above all urgent not to think of it as a "moment," historical or otherwise . . .

Index